RETRO style

the '50s look for today's home

RETRO style

the '50s look for today's home

MARION HASLAM

photography by Sue Wilson
styling by Beth Evans

CONTENTS

Introduction

The 1950s were an amazing and exciting decade for change and creativity. After ten years of hardship, deprivation, and austerity during World War II and the post-war '40s, the '50s dawned as a bright new era. The American designer Raymond Loewy coined the phrase "blue skies design" to describe the yearning optimism and feel-good factor that pervaded the early years of the decade. The amazing transformation was due mainly to four factors: great leaps forward in manufacturing processes; peacetime inventions and scientific discoveries; the growth of consumerism as people had more disposable income and wartime rationing was lifted; a public craving for color, fun, modernity, and a new look for a new generation; and finally, a new global awareness of popular culture through the growing influence of television and film.

Nowhere is this change more apparent than in the interior style and homes of the '50s. And to prove that what goes around comes around, as we enter a new millennium, this contemporary mood and desire for individuality resurfaces to give a new twist on '50s retro style. This book explores decorative styles based on the designs and colors of that era. However, this is not a time-warped trip down memory lane, but a fresh combination of elements right for today's living.

Until recently the '50s were a forgotten era—too close to be history, yet too long ago to be seen as modern. However, with the recent interest in '60s pop and '70s psychedelia, designers have now switched their attention to the '50s and, like a Pandora's box, it has opened to reveal a host of treasures, many surprises and, like every era, some real humdingers. And why is retro style right for today? Well, '50s style was all about being contemporary, having fun, and celebrating a bright, new decade. What better recipe for a new century?

WHAT MAKES A CLASSIC DESIGN?

What is incredible about some '50s designs is their longevity. For example, much of the original '50s furniture featured here is still in production today. In fact, to many people the furniture looks so modern, they are thought to be contemporary designs, not items approaching their half-century anniversary. A good example is Arne Jacobsen's Ant chair (see page 77), which has been constantly manufactured since its launch in 1952; other pieces such as Robin Day's Forum range (see page 10) have recently gone back into production, as manufacturers and retailers reappraise the classic designs lodged in their archives.

MAKE DO AND MEND

The good things about '50s design are its affordability and adaptability. Whether choosing vintage or modern versions, many '50s pieces are still remarkably inexpensive. Many people who furnished their homes for the first time in the '50s do not regard retro items as collectibles or classics, so when attics undergo spring-cleaning, items regularly turn up in junk shops or flea markets at prices that don't require a second mortgage. Also, this was a decade when mass production of domestic accessories was at an all-time high, so there is a large amount of retro material on the market.

This was also an era with a great entrepreneurial spirit. This cavalier attitude was combined with a "make do and mend" philosophy inbred by a decade of austerity in the '40s. As a result, many retro decorating ideas are inexpensive to try. All of the projects in this book embody this spirit. None requires expensive materials or great expertise, just a willingness to invest a few hours of time to create individual and quirky accessories for your home.

And lest you think that retro is simply a folksy, rose-tinted trip into the past and therefore not suitable for switched-on decorators of today, look at the opposite page to see that retro is relevant to today's style. Browse through the pages at the end of this section to get you in the mood, and then pick or combine the styles that best define your way of living, and remember that retro is certainly not nostalgia per se, but is definitely a cocktail of the best of the '50s and today, shaken and stirred with a slice of style.

RIGHT Classic '50s elements for contemporary style today: stunning color, bold upholstery shapes, and sleek storage.

HOMES IN THE '50S

"It's hard for anyone who wasn't around at the time to understand that there just wasn't the choice available. Nothing was wasted and we had to improvise if we wanted anything special. I was longing for some colored china." *Mavis Haslam*

This is one of my mother's memories from the early 50s, when my parents married and set up home. More than at any other time, home design in the '40s and '50s received a radical shake-up. During World War II, one in three homes in Britain was bomb-damaged and a further half a million totally destroyed. Add to this the two million demobbed servicemen and -women and the huge increase in the birth rate, and the result was an urgent need to address housing issues. As a

LEFT More informal lifestyles meant a rise in the popularity of mix-and-match casual china. Advances in manufacturing also enabled potteries to experiment with more unusual shapes, such as squares and triangles.

result, the government started a program of building 300,000 new homes a year, and created five new towns according to the "garden city" principles established earlier in the century. These carefully planned urban models pioneered the inclusion of open spaces, tree-lined roads, a lower density of housing, and accessible schools, shops, and community facilities. Such ideas were intended to promote a feeling of pride and neighborliness in these instant communities. There was an overwhelming desire to rebuild a bright new Britain in which to live and bring up a new generation untouched by the horror of two world wars.

However, these utopian ideals took some time to come to fruition as the building and manufacturing industries had to start up again, having switched much of their production to the war effort. As an interim measure, more than 153,000 temporary bungalows or prefabs (they were made of prefabricated elements that were simply slotted together) were constructed. Intended to last for just a few years while the rebuilding of Britain took place, more than 50,000 still exist today. They included many features that characterize mid-century homes—open living spaces rather than a warren of tiny rooms, large picture windows, indoor bathrooms, electricity, and good insulation. All in all, these little chalets looked and seemed like delightful holiday homes in comparison to the unmodernized Victorian homes many of their owners had previously lived in.

The more permanent postwar homes also reflected changes in society: There was very little domestic help so homes had to

be easier to keep clean, especially as some women wanted to work part-time; a more relaxed way of living including a greater amount of home entertainment through the radio and television; more leisure time resulting in growing interest in home improvements and gardening; and finally an emotional and practical desire for bright, new homes in contrast to the previous dark decades. The mock period effects that had been common in prewar homes were abandoned in place of a new honesty in architecture, with natural wood and white painted boarding, simple porches, and casement windows being common features. This hunger for newness, modernity, and color permeated down from the architecture to the teacup, and designers in the '50s sought to keep the public appetite satisfied with a constant stream of contemporary furniture and accessories.

These values are little changed fifty years on—the interest in home design has never been greater. Shopping is a leisure activity and, as style magazines quip, "staying in is the new going out." As we start a new millennium, there is a desire like never before to cocoon ourselves and enjoy living in relaxing, individual homes that efficiently cater to our multifaceted lives.

AMERICAN HOMES

By contrast, homes in the United States had already been incorporating these contemporary features throughout the '40s. Unlike Britain, dubbed "the land of beginning again" by Juliet Gardiner (*From the Bomb to the Beatles*), there was no need to rebuild towns and cities devastated by war. America entered the '50s economically stable. The modern look for homes was often called "the West Coast look" as it originated in California. It featured a wide use of natural materials such as wood, glass, and stone. There was an emphasis on family life, and an embracing of new technology such as laminated surfaces, televisions, and washing machines. No wonder Britain wanted to emulate America, as it seemed to be a country where one could have it all and could have it *now*.

BELOW Uncompromisingly modern, Robin Day's Forum upholstery successfully straddles fifty years of changing styles.

THE FESTIVAL OF BRITAIN

One of the launchpads for the New Look decade was the Festival of Britain, staged in 1951. This key event was referred to as "a tonic to the nation," a phrase coined by Sir Gerald Barry, the Festival's Director General. The festival was the climax of a series of morale-boosting consumer exhibitions organized after the war. After a decade of "making do" and "keeping your chin up," Herbert Morrison, the government minister responsible for the festival's organization, announced that "we ought to do something jolly . . . we need something to give Britain a lift." Originally planned as a trade exhibition, it

"I remember the 1953 Ideal Home Exhibition, and drooling at the stuff on display. Everyone wanted something different. However, most things were in short supply and went for export. If you wanted to buy, you simply put your name on a waiting list and had to wait, sometimes for up to a year." *Joe Haslam*

soon developed into a consumer fair intended to display the best of new designs, available to a public hungry for products for their homes. On a more propagandist level, it was a visible display of a new optimism at home and abroad. It was a massive undertaking for a country still in the grips of rationing and massive economic debt. As it was intended to showcase the talents of young designers and architects and a new style, Modernism, many new designs were commissioned. Temporary structures such as the Skylon and Dome of Discovery were intended to dazzle the public gripped by a space-and-science frenzy. The Skylon was part modern sculpture, part structural engineering—a huge rocket-shaped structure suspended and supported by wires that were almost invisible. The Dome of Discovery featured different areas encompassing the arts, sciences, and humanities.

It was a great success—more than eight million visitors flocked to the site on the South Bank in London. The designs of the festival filtered into mass production and reverberated like aftershocks throughout the decade. It opened the public's eyes to a bright new look and although it was a great launchpad for young designers such as Terence Conran and Lucienne and Robin Day, the overall success of the festival was to set in motion a collective modern look.

RIGHT The ultimate '50s icon is the Roberts Revival radio. Transistor radios appealed in to teenagers and adults alike, and came in a range of fun and flirty colors.

Optimism

1952 Immigration and Naturalization Act signed

1953 Dwight D. Eisenhower becomes President

1953 John F. Kennedy marries Jacqueline Bouvier

1954 Supreme Court rules against segregation in Brown vs Board of Education of Topeka, Kansas

1955 Senate votes to censure Joseph McCarthy

1955 Rosa Parks refuses to surrender her bus seat to a white man

1955 Guggenheim Museum opens in New York City

NEW ERA

BLUE SKIES DESIGN

FRESH START

CELEBRATION

Suburbia and family life

1950 *The Lone Ranger* series begins

1951 The first supermarket chain opens

1951 *I Love Lucy* sitcom begins

1952 Utility furniture scheme ends

1954 *Father Knows Best* sitcom starts

1955 *The Adventures of Ozzie and Harriet* sitcom starts

1955 *Captain Kangaroo* children's television program begins

1956 First Teflon nonstick frying pan made in the United States

1959 *The Twilight Zone* series begins

1959 Austin Mini car launched

1959 Birth of Barbie dolls

Gaiety

1952 Marilyn Monroe inspires the "sweater girl" look

1954 *Miss America* pageant first televised

1955 Disneyland opens in California

1955 Ann Landers' advice column first appears in newspapers

1957 Frisbee invented

1959 Hawaii becomes the fiftieth U.S. state

MIX 'N' MATCH

PLASTIC FANTASTIC

COCKTAIL TIME

HIS AND HERS

ATOMIC

MICRO, MACRO

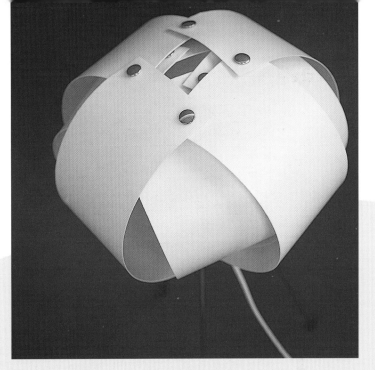

Space race and nuclear age

1950 Point Four Program launched to provide technological aid to developing nations

1950 Outbreak of the Korean War (ends in 1953)

1951 First commercial manufacture of computers

1952 The United States detonates H bomb

1953 DNA molecule discovered

1954 Robert Oppenheimer dismissed from Manhattan Project

1955 Polio vaccine introduced

1956 Calder Hall nuclear power station opens

1956 Suez crisis

1957 Russian satellite Sputnik I circles the globe; Sputnik II launches a dog into space

1958 Inauguration of NASA

1958 Explorer I, the first U.S. satellite launched

1959 Soviet rocket photographs the far side of the moon

Rock and roll

1951 The film *A Street Car Named Desire* released

1951 *Superman* television series starts

1952 Contraceptive pill first manufactured

1953 The James Bond era starts with *Casino Royale*

1954 Audrey Hepburn wins Oscar for *Roman Holiday*

1955 Little Richard releases *Tutti Frutti*

1955 *Rebel Without a Cause* and James Dean's death hit the headlines

1955 Chuck Berry releases *Maybelline*

1956 Elvis Presley signs record deal with RCA

1957 First pocket-size transistor radio marketed by Sony

TEENAGER

JUKEBOX

Consumer age

1950   Commercial television starts in the United States

1950   Diners Club, the first credit card with a plastic and metallic strip, launched

1952   Sugar Smacks cereal introduced

1953   Color television demonstrated in New York

1953   Chevrolet Corvette launched

1954   M&M peanuts introduced

1957   Boeing 707 passenger jet makes its inaugural flight

1957   Pampers disposable diapers debuts

NEW-AND-IMPROVED

STREAMLINED

CONVENIENCE

NEW MATERIALS

"The only limits are as always those of vision."

James Broughton, American poet and playwright

The '50s were dominated by manufacturing advances and scientific developments. No other decade had seen such an explosion of synthetic materials available to consumers. If it was synthetic, it was modern, and if it was modern, it was a craved-for commodity. The magic words were *nylon*, *laminate*, *PVC*, *molded plastic*, *melamine*, *plywood*, and *vinyl*— wonder materials for a modern age.

Less glamorous but equally important, plastics technology helped develop new paints and adhesives. In the '50s, many of the new materials were affordable to the majority for the first time. They were also flexible to use for home improvements enthusiasts, easy to care for and colorful—winning combinations in a booming consumer market. So for a truly contemporary home, use the best of today's new materials and for a retro touch, look at '50s styling and colors for a happy fusion of retro modern and millennium modern.

ABOVE Get into the groove with this shiny chrome and vinyl '50s-style diner stool.

LEFT Plastic fantastic—everyday beakers look as elegant in plastic as they would in bone china, with the advantage of being a lot more practical.

FAR LEFT Now you see it. Perspex is an ideal material for space-enhancing furniture such as this transparent bedside table.

Plastic fantastic

When you think '50s, you automatically picture plastics—everything from squeeze ketchup bottles in the shape of tomatoes to stringy bead curtains. Maybe cutting edge from a scientific point of view, but hardly in design terms. Plastic equals tacky and vulgar, hardly elements for a stylish home today. Not so. If you look around, even the most design-led homes have plastics everywhere.

The trick is to decide which route you wish to follow. Colorful kitsch is the easiest and cheapest to achieve by scouting around hardware shops and discount stores. Look for crazily colored kitchenware, canary yellow is the preferred shade for washing-up bowls, with sky-blue trashcans and shocking pink scrubbing brushes for contrast. Add melamine tableware, inflatable egg cups, and a PVC tablecloth, and suddenly your home is a brighter, cheerier place.

If, on the other hand, no color is more your color, stick to acrylics and polypropylene accessories in subtle colors and frosted finishes. Polypropylene seems to be the plastic of the millennium and is used by manufacturers everywhere for furniture and housewares. It can also be bought by the sheet from good art shops and bent, folded, or riveted fairly easily into a variety of products, such as lights, storage, and desk accessories. Acrylic is most commonly seen around the home as cutlery handles, clip-top storage jars and clear picture frames, the latter often simply fastened at each corner with metal prongs. All these items can give a "soft, modern" look to a home and look great when combined with classic '50s furniture and homewares. So for an authentic retro look, pile on the plastic.

TOP LEFT Woven plastic strips form a strong yet light magazine rack.

BELOW LEFT Plastics revolutionized '50s homes. Brightly colored housewares were an inexpensive way to brighten up kitchens and family mealtimes.

RIGHT CLOCKWISE FROM TOP LEFT Inexpensive scrubbing brushes manage to make washing up less of a chore.

A house is not a home without a novelty tissue box holder.

Polka dot beakers can be mixed and not matched, and used to hold juice, or even pencils or toothbrushes.

A low wattage polypropylene lamp gives out a gentle glow, and is ideal for a child's bedroom.

Plastic pastel cutlery should not be kept just for summer picnics, they are also fun for jello and ice-cream parties, or relaxed takeaway suppers.

Encourage youngsters to eat up their porridge with these color-coded baby bowls.

No aspiring hostess with the mostest would consider the table properly dressed without a holder for the chutney spoon.

The interlocking levels of this stacking wine rack create an undulating structure. The mineral water bottles further emphasize the many different plastics available today.

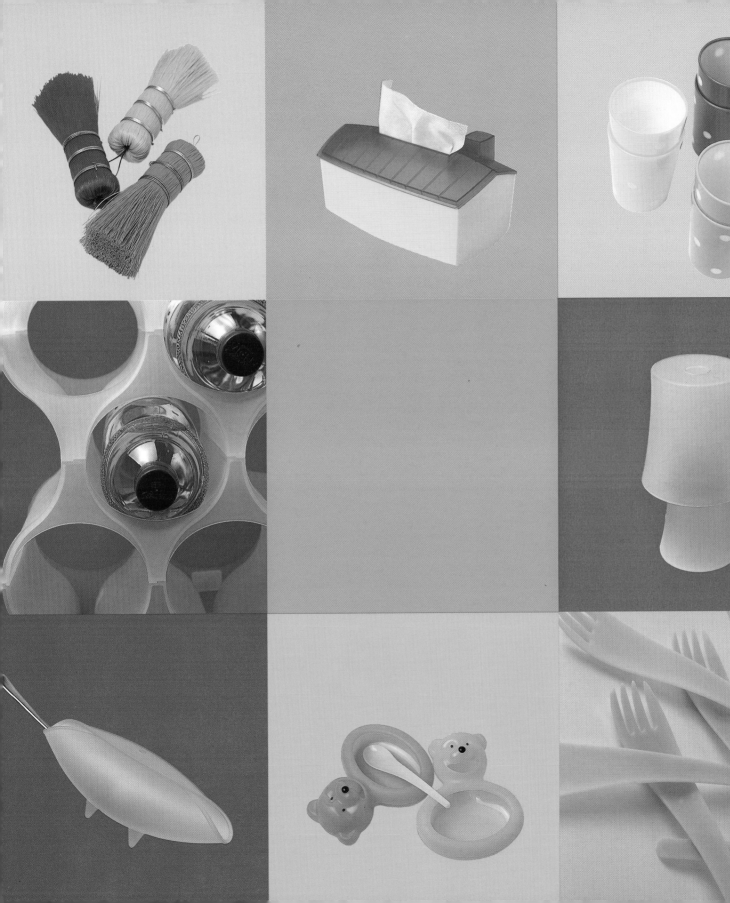

Plywood

Ever since Michael Thonet first steam-bent his classic beech bentwood chairs in 1859, the technique of manipulated wooden furniture made from veneers has been intriguing furniture designers. Plywood is a generic term describing thin layers of wood glued together at right angles to produce a strong yet lightweight construction material. The inner core of plywood is made from the less expensive wood and may be up to nine layers thick; the outer layer or "face" is covered with

a veneer. The resulting wood can be molded and hydraulically pressed into complex yet simple forms, constructed from a single piece of ply without joins.

In the early part of the twentieth century, the use of ply in furniture manufacturing was still very labor-intensive. However, during World War II, plywood was widely used for military purposes, particularly in Mosquito bomber aircraft due to its lightness. Because of this, advances were made in manufacturing and suddenly designers were hailing it as "the new wood." Plywood can be made from a variety of woods, so designs abound in beech, birch, ash, walnut, and cherry.

One of the designers, best known for his revolutionary use of plywood and its manipulation into three-dimensional shaped forms, is Charles Eames (see page 70). Finnish designer Alvar Aalto was bending plywood in one direction, but Eames managed to mold it into complex multidirectional curves. This gave him an enormous freedom and flexibility to design comfortable chairs to fit the curvature of the body. Eames's brilliance with plywood was a result of his technical understanding of this material. After his success with his first ply design in 1940, he continued to experiment with plywood and some of his most successful designs include the DCM, LCM, and LCW chairs. In the '50s, Eames's classic forms proved a catalyst to designers worldwide.

Plywood is most appropriate for clean and simple designs which is why it appealed so much to the modern school of product designers in the '50s. Today, there is a resurgence of interest in the material,

particularly as it is environmentally friendly, effectively using 90 to 95 percent of the timber available and creating very little waste during its manufacture.

ABOVE If you buy only one thing in plywood, make it a quirky magazine rack-cum-cocktail cabinet perching delicately on thin legs.

LEFT Just as in the '50s, modern plywood designs are based equally on form and structure. The gently rounded corners of this stool play up the grain of the birch wood.

RIGHT The butterfly stool in the foreground was created by Japanese designer, Sori Yanagi in 1954. It epitomizes the simplicity of the best plywood designs—two identical L-shapes held together by a single brass rod and two screws. Still in production today, it words equally well as a side table.

On the book: MODERN ART

Laminate—the wipe-clean wonder

was the early '50s when it was used in schools, diners, and railroad cars because of its wipe-clean nature and cigarette-proof surface. Of the six million American homes built in the immediate postwar period, two million had Formica countertops in their kitchens.

In Britain, too, Formica was hailed as a "new" modern material. Homemakers couldn't get enough of the stuff and it was used throughout the home. New developments in adhesives made it easy to use and combined with its bright, gay colors, geometric and abstract surface designs proved a winning combination. Furniture manufacturers emphasized its easy-to-clean surface and flexibility as a contemporary decorating material. As a result, sales boomed.

While home owners today may regard Formica and laminates as an old hat, like many other mid-century fads, the material has updated itself for a new millennium with veneer-type finishes for flooring, making it ideal for kitchens and bathrooms. Contemporary furniture designers are now using laminates as an integral element of their designs rather than simply a surface covering.

LEFT Stark and simple, these laminate chairs do not try to hide the nuts and bolts of this construction. The shaped seat enables them to be stacked when not in use.

BELOW This sofa's fluid lines make the most of malleable plywood and laminate.

Laminate was the forerunner of MDF (medium density fiberboard)—an all-purpose wonder product loved by decorators everywhere. Just like MDF, laminates were fashioned into furniture and accessories throughout the home. They were often highly patterned or colored and were oh so modern.

The most famous laminate of them all has to be Formica, the brand name of a sheet laminate made from resin-impregnated decorative paper on a core of Kraft paper, first manufactured in the United States in 1914. Originally invented as an electrical insulator, Formica evolved into decorative sheets as printing processes improved. This enabled the Formica company to produced laminates resembling wood grain and marble. As well as aesthetics, Formica's main selling point was its durability and reasonable price. Its golden age

Synthetic fabrics—drip-dry and easy care

In the '50s new advances in fabric technology (many as a result of wartime military developments) meant that stores were suddenly awash with shiny, brightly colored "wonder fabrics" for use in the home. Acetate, rayon, nylon, polyester, Terylene—all were seen as the "way forward."

No longer would housewives have to contend with drying and ironing heavy cotton or linen sheets—the future was filled with drip-dry, non-iron nylon in '50s pastel colors. With hindsight, anyone that has experienced sleeping between such slippery surfaces, which rapidly induce a sauna-type "glow," is no doubt grateful that this trend has passed and we have rediscovered the crispness and comfort of sleeping next to natural fabrics. When synthetics are used, such as in polyester-filled duvets, a natural cotton cover means that warmth and comfort can be combined.

At the time, however, synthetic bed linen was a real boon. Combined with the new washer-dryer, wash days were no longer dreaded. Manufacturers played on this "no-drudge" housework by advertising their washing machines with glamorous models in cocktail dresses, perfectly manicured and coiffeured.

Today, synthetic materials have all the advantages and none of the drawbacks. Many synthetic materials now used in the home have developed from performance fashion fabrics—neoprene and polar fleece being two of the most popular. Neoprene, formerly only used for wet suits, is the fashionable new wonder fabric now being used for bath mats, wine coolers, cushions, and anything else designers can think of. Some products clearly make use of its insulating properties and ability to shrug off water. Others are more concerned with its visual and tactile appeal. Fleece has also made the move indoors and is marvelous for wonderfully warm soft furnishings. Easy to sew, it is ideal for blankets, throws, and cushion covers.

Another material great for quick cover-ups in family kitchens and children's rooms is PVC-coated fabric. For tablecloths it needs no hemming. However, it can also be ideal for sewing into hanging storage for toys or clothes. Finally, no bathroom is complete without a vinyl or nylon shower curtain. For many years good design and shower curtains were two polar concepts. However, in recent years several companies have realized that bathrooms need not be just hygienic havens, but can also be fun, relaxing rooms. Whether you are after the wackiness of hundreds of cavorting goldfish, the galactic millennium-chic appeal of holograms, or simple graphic impact, there is a shower curtain design just right for you. Some shower curtains even have the added bonus of sewn-in pockets—a boon for bathrooms where storage space for shower gels and scrubbing brushes is at a premium.

BELOW Splash-happy PVC fabrics and a rubber floor ensure a squeaky clean kitchen with minimum fuss.

VINYL MAGAZINE HOLDERS

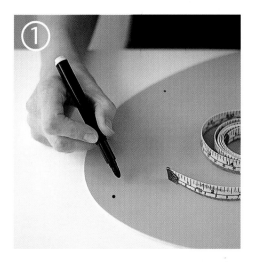

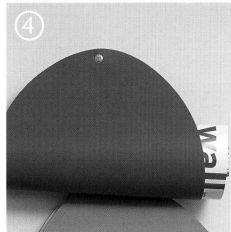

Keep favorite magazines close to hand with this vinyl magazine holder. Simply add more sections as your collection grows.

1. Using the fiber-tipped pen, mark a dot at each end of the placemat $5/8$in. in from the edge.

2. Carefully heat a skewer over a gas flame and when hot, pierce the mat on the dot. Repeat at the other end of the placemat.

3. Following the manufacturer's instructions with the eyelet kit, attach and hammer a metal eyelet around the holes at the ends of the placemat.

4. Using the drill, drill six holes in the wall in a vertical row $5^{1}/_{2}$in. apart and insert a rawl plug into each hole. Screw the cup hooks into the rawl plugs. Fold over each magazine holder to form a sling and hang.

YOU WILL NEED

Six flexible foam-backed placemats, each 12 × 18in.
Black fiber-tipped pen
Ruler or tape measure
Metal skewer
Chrome or brass $1/4$in. eyelet kit
Hammer
Wood drill
Six small metal cup hooks and rawl plugs

TIPS

- For a subtle look, use placemats all in the same color.
- If you cannot find vinyl placemats, you could use vinyl flooring or polypropylene sheets, cut into ovals.
- Simply add more holders depending on the number of magazines you want on display.
- To keep the holder portable, attach the cup hooks to a length of MDF at least 14in. wide painted to match or contrast with the holders. The MDF can then be rested at an angle against the wall.

27

COLOR

"There are times to be gentle with color,
times to be brave, but never a time to be dull."

Jane Faulkener, Australian writer

After the general grayness, both literally and emotionally, of the '40s, the '50s dawned as a bright new era—gaudy, sophisticated, modern, and above all colorful. Advances in manufacturing meant that color as a commodity was available in a variety of decorative materials such as paint, wallpaper, laminate, and vinyl. Decorating your home today using retro colors as inspiration has never been easier. Whatever your personal preferences, there are sure to be combinations that appeal. Fifties color palettes are an effective shorthand for the styles and fads of the decade—understand these and the rest of the retro world slips neatly into place.

There are essentially three definitive retro color palettes: Scandinavian, pastel, and modern. Fifties consumers tended to fall into one category or another, but today's eclectic decorator is more confident at combining elements from each. In fact, this mixing up

and adaptation is necessary to create an original decorative scheme and not simply a pastiche of the past. Pastels combined with Scandinavian simplicity create a sharper, contemporary look while the use of natural tones prevalent in the Scandinavian palette soften the modern colors and create a scheme that is easier to live with. Hue, texture, and finish are equally important considerations. Fifties paint finishes were much more limited than those available today. To achieve an authentic look, eggshell and flat paints are ideal. To reflect the light in this matt environment, use shiny or brushed chrome details, glass, and glossy ceramics. Plastic accessories also add to the sheen.

Unlike more historical color schemes, there is little archive material showing paint colors available in the '50s. At the beginning of the decade, color was rationed: white, cream, and black being available in gloss finish and a

powder distemper to which colors were added. However, as the restrictions on domestic paint manufacture were lifted, home improvements mania took off. Flat oil paints were used in place of today's emulsions. They required thinning with linseed oil and white spirit before application because as one British manufacturer, Walpamur, stated in its color card, "Muromatte is supplied in a rather stout consistency." While the standard color chart now appears rather conservative, a second fifty-fifty chart (see page 129) demonstrates how the colors can be combined by intrepid home decorators to produce more subtle shades. Since the '50s color palette included every color in the spectrum, today's retro devotee can pick and chose at will.

LEFT Pick a color, any color. As the Phoenix plywood chair is available in over twenty colors, there's sure to be at least one that you like.

Pastel perfection

"A world full of color is synonymous with paradise."

*Friedensreich Hundertwasser,
German architect*

Think of the '50s and a pastel color scheme immediately springs to mind—with images of milk bars, sherbet dips, and multicolored, multi-layered ice-cream sundaes. These light, fresh, optimistic colors were a youthful reaction to the dull, muted colors of the previous decade. Even the names used to describe the colors seem gentle and nostalgic—lemon yellow, duck-egg blue, pistachio, mint, eau-de-nil, pearl gray, almond pink, milk white, lilac, powder blue, leaf green, and fresh cream.

The postwar baby boom meant that nurseries became a temple to pastels, the color chosen strictly determined by the sex of the child, powder blue or rose pink or if in doubt, lemon yellow. Like today, interior trends followed close on the heels of fashion—pastels were popular for knitted twinsets teamed with Capri pants and ballet slippers.

For '50s interiors, pastels were most evident in what were often perceived as the feminine areas of the house—the bedroom and kitchen. In bedrooms, new nylon sheets, fluffy bedroom rugs, and kidney-shaped dressing tables were usually pastel. In kitchens, Formica became readily available, so laminated tables and chairs were popular in sorbet colors.

The availability of domestic appliances in a range of colors is not a new development. In the '50s, manufacturers such as Westinghouse and Morphy Richards recognized the marketing potential of the housewife as a customer. By producing irons in lemon yellow, they became a fashionable home accessory rather than an appliance for doing the daily household chores. In the '80s and early '90s white goods returned to being white or sometimes beige as they were "functional machines." However, after fifty years, there is now a revival for the kettle, toaster, and hand blender as fashionable kitchen accessories. Combining modern technology with rounded, retro styling, pastels have once again proven that feminine color follows swiftly after form and function.

So how does one achieve the sorbet look today without degenerating into a saccharine sweetness? Well for starters, today's canny home decorator is more streetwise than the

'50s consumer who was so hungry for what was new she slavishly followed the advice of advertisers and women's magazines. Today's look is more eclectic. For example, combine the best of today's efficient kitchen with some charm or color from the '50s. Today's birch or pale maple kitchen may be unfitted, but it's always ergonomic. By adding a retro kitchen cupboard with patchwork paintwork, or four Danish laminated chairs in different colors, the effect remains unfussy but fun. To finish, add some acrylic or polypropylene accessories, plus a little shiny chrome or galvanized steel and presto, it's millennium chic meets retro style.

Pastels of the '50s are ideal as flirty bedroom color schemes. In recent years design companies have rediscovered how fresh combinations of lilac, green, lavender, and blue can look. To achieve the retro look, glossy white boards replace the linoleum of yesteryear, the hardness balanced by ultrasoft rugs for toes to sink into. Crisp white cotton sheets, rose-print duvets, and piles of cushions made from vintage fabric scraps provide a powder-puff-boudoir look and a calm retreat from the harsh modern world outside.

For an eclectic mix, it is best not to coordinate colors exactly, or patterns perfectly. A potpourri of patterns such as a stenciled floor

(see pages 40–41) together with tiny
ginghams and overblown florals will give the
look of a herbaceous border. For more
sophisticated style, steer clear of patterns
altogether and choose luxurious fabrics such
as pure linen curtains or bed linen, and raw silk
throws trimmed with a wide satin border.
Cushions in crisp black-and-white ticking or
sharper colors such as chartreuse or deep lilac
prevent the look from becoming too sweet.
And just to emphasize that this is retro style
with a twist, the finishing touch for today's
home owner is more likely to be linen pajamas
and flip-flops adorned with perky pink
carnations, rather than a slinky housecoat and
stiletto mules.

In a living room, plump velvet cushions in
raspberry, leaf green, mint, and pink can
make even the most austere sofa more
inviting, and prove that pastels aren't just for
the girls. Give pastels more bite by painting
the different sections of modular storage units
in a selection of colors, propped by a few
well-chosen possessions. Also remember that
pastels look their best in a soft diffused light
so hang organza panels or blinds at the
windows. Complete with plenty of wall lamps
and chrome or aluminium up lighters to wash
the walls and ceiling with gentle light, and
Noguchi-style table lamps for accent lighting.

LEFT Kitchen clock with an integral timer,
made of bakelite, one of the classic plastics
of the twentieth century.

ABOVE LEFT Slender ceramic vases in pale
turquoise would look terrific filled with a
few flowers in delicate sorbet colors.

RIGHT A pine headboard painted lilac
complements the duck-egg blue bed linen
with perky zinnias and polka dots.

The Scandinavian look

Of all the color schemes popular in the '50s, the Scandinavian palette, or "contemporary look" as it was then known, is definitely the most sophisticated and probably the easiest to live with.

The look is neither the Gustavian nor summer house "Swedish style," which is so often described in interior design books today. Instead, it is a palette of discreet luxury whose colors are derived not just from paint or wallpapers, but also from the natural materials used in house interiors.

Unlike Britain, which has always preferred to cocoon a house with wall-to-wall carpeting and cozy curtains to prevent heat loss, Scandinavian countries have concentrated on energy-efficient house designs. This approach

has enabled them to sport bare wood floors and simple window treatments such as wooden Venetian blinds or shutters. The Scandinavian look was designed to be complementary to these natural materials and textures. Predominant paint colors include all shades of brown, cream, gray, and green.

> "The Scandinavians exploited the warm, visual and tactile appeal of natural materials and favored discreet, soft contoured forms."
>
> *Philippe Garner, author,*
> Twentieth Century Furniture

During the '50s, Denmark was particularly important for furniture design and production. Designers such Hans Wegner, Poul Henningsen, Finn Juhl, and Arne Jacobsen worked with ash, beech, birch, oak, and teak, either as solid wood or as ply sheets.

Upholstery varied from interwoven leather or hemp braids used as chair slings to densely woven cane or subtle woven fabrics in a single color. Interior design picked up on the subtlety of these textures and colors.

The Scandinavian look was particularly popular in the United States as it worked well in the contemporary homes built of wood and stone that were all the rage. In the late '50s, this

more subdued palette of tobacco brown and mossy green gained popularity in Britain, possibly as a reaction against the bright candy-floss colors and strident modernity of earlier years.

Scandinavian is an easy retro colorway to incorporate in any contemporary interior. The classic elements are wood, natural textures, and soft (but not subdued) colors. The emphasis is on a tactile environment as well as a purely visual one.

For a true Scandinavian feel, furniture and accessories should be pared down to a few key pieces. The look is more about space and light than clutter and chaotic color schemes.

LEFT Scandinavian colors are typified by their subtlety and depth of tone. These moss green, mushroom, claret, and soft blue mugs provide an excellent starting point for a '50s-style interior.

RIGHT The Scandinavian color palette is full of contrasting natural tones, with a healthy dose of monochromes. The style should embody comfort with a tactile mix and focus on space and light.

PAGE 32 Pastels crop up in every room of the retro home, from furniture to tableware, accessories, and even food. Regardless of color, pastels work happily together, and can be sharpened up with crisp white and chrome.

PAGE 33 A lightweight crescent-shaped table in a gentle shade of lilac is ideal for the bedtime cocoa mug.

Modern times

"A young newly married couple will most likely desire a bright, lively atmosphere throughout their newly furnished home and will tend to use bright colors everywhere. But too much stimulating color is restless and tiring and a modicum of restraint should be exercised."

As this extract from a '50s decorating manual confirms, of all the color schemes, modern is the most gaudy and striking. It is based around the three primary colors of red, yellow, and blue with splashes of black, white, and gray.

The colors used were often the undiluted pure pigment, so the contrast and impact was at its most extreme. The plain upholstery fabric used on contemporary designs such as the Egg and Swan chairs (see pages 76-77) was usually a plain weave so there was no dilution of the visual impact. Laminates from companies such as Formica and Wilson Art occasionally had a subtle textured design, and small kitchen tables with bright red or yellow glossy wipe-clean surfaces were common. A modern color scheme is probably the most demanding to live with because of the strength of the colors. However, it can also be energizing. The easiest way to ensure that such intense colors work well together is to use the same intensity such as pillar-box red, canary yellow, and electric blue—shades that are equally strong. If this combination is too lively, the modern look can also be achieved with more muted colors—a softer tomato red will be balanced by a slate blue and a lemon yellow. White can be added to the pure colors so they become a shade lighter (but not as pale as pastels). Similarly, by adding a little black, the colors change to ruby, mustard yellow, and midnight blue and are equally effective.

As with any decorating scheme, the colors do not have to be used in even proportions—it is far easier to decide on a main color and then use additional colors to complement it, perhaps with one used sparingly as a sharp accent. This concern over how to use color was emphasized in practical decorating pamphlets of the '50s, which were really quite condemning of the lack of taste shown by home decorators:

"For some years now it has been fashionable to decorate the walls of a room in different colors. Like all innovations which 'catch on,' however, this device has been grossly overdone, often with deplorable results—as when all four walls are in different colors. It is unfortunate that this idea has been applied with so little understanding and lack of taste, that it has now lost favor in the most discriminating circles."
The Wall Paper Manufacturers Limited

Modern schemes are ideally suited to more active rooms or areas that are passed through quickly, such as hallways and landings.

LEFT Turquoise provides an energizing flash of color in this light and airy room. The fluid lines of the Noguchi table complement the solid blocks of color on the black sofa. Carefully placed satsuma-colored cushions and a retro style floor lamp are important finishing touches.

ABOVE RIGHT Small doses of modern color such as this laminate tray and melamine teacup look striking. The colors should be intense and undiluted.

RIGHT An uncompromisingly contemporary table is balanced by the bold shape and color of the glass vase and Gerbera daisies.

Research has shown that the best color for a front door is a rich blue, so why not carry the modern retro look into the hall with a checkerboard-tiled floor in white and black, with royal blue or egg-yolk-yellow walls. Such a scheme would look stunning, and would need little propping with furniture or accessories—maybe just a red Ericofon telephone set on a spindly white metal garden chair.

The larger the room, the easier it is to incorporate modern colors, especially if they are separated by other elements such as rough brick walls, large windows, high ceilings, or concrete or wooden flooring. Loft-style apartments respond well to intense colors due to their vastness and rawness. A large painted screen used as a room divider, painted wall canvases, or a solid-color rug in a living area will provide strong punctuation marks and help to create areas of focus, whereas paler colors will simply not have the necessary

impact. Alternatively, more temporary spots of color can be achieved using fold-up Butterfly chairs (see page 73) which have an airiness to them due to their slim metal frame, an assortment of Ant chairs around a wooded table (see page 77), or with a single to-die-for upholstered chair in an eye-popping color.

And for those of us who live in smaller, box-like homes with low ceilings—how can modern colors be incorporated? It is here that the restraint so urged by the '50s manufacturers kicks in. For example, in a bedroom measuring 12 × 12 feet there are three options.

The first is to throw out the rule book, which encourages pale colors to enlarge spaces, and paint all the walls in a gloriously deep tone. This will give the room a presence and vitality that no amount of peach haze or barley white will ever achieve. The floor should be as pale

as possible to reflect the light and the furniture kept to a minimum so that the color can take center stage. A few well-chosen accessories in a contrasting color, such as glass vases, abstract art, or a strictly controlled collection of kitsch, are all that's needed as accents.

Alternatively, paint or wallpaper one wall in a strong color and do the remaining walls in a soft gray or other lighter tone. In a bedroom, this can look particularly effective if the wall chosen is the one behind the bed—this gives the appearance of an oversized headboard (plus, if you still need some persuading, the wall is not visible when you are lying in bed!).

The third option is to have white walls and put the color on the floor. The variety of floor paints now available makes this scheme extremely inexpensive as there is no need for expensive or long-term carpeting. As the color is concentrated on the floor, there is more opportunity to show less restraint with window treatments or lighting, as they will be set against the neutral foil of the walls. This is probably the best option if you have a large collection of accessories, books, or pictures to be displayed.

If you live in a rented apartment and are unable to decorate the walls or floors, don't despair. Inject modern color into a neutral space with vibrant upholstery, or throws and accessories, which you can take with you when you move on.

LEFT Lipstick red, magenta, and purple happily coexist in a living room when they are surrounded with plenty of white and natural wood to give the separate colors room to breathe.

STENCILED FLOOR

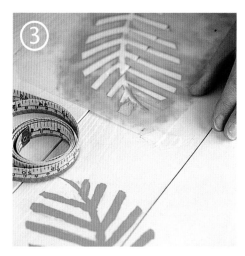

Give an old wooden floor a new lease of life with a coat of paint and a jazzy stencil.

1. Prepare the boards by hammering down or screwing in any nails which are standing proud. Vacuum, then wash the floor to remove any dust and grease. Prime bare boards with wood primer and allow to dry. Paint the boards with one or two coats of satinwood paint.

2. Draw the leaf design onto paper with thick black pen. Place the stencil plastic over the design and secure on a cutting board with masking tape. Using a craft knife, carefully cut out the stencil.

3. Calculate the positioning of the stencil on the boards. Use a tape measure or ruler if you wish the designs to appear at set intervals and, if necessary, bear in mind where any large pieces of furniture will be placed.

4. Secure the stencil to the floor with masking tape. Apply the paint to the stencil with a small brush. Carefully remove the stencil, clean any paint from the underside and reposition it where necessary. Leave the floor to dry before varnishing.

YOU WILL NEED

Hammer or screwdriver
Wood primer
Paintbrush
Satinwood paint in base color
Paper
Thick black marker pen
Stencil plastic
Cutting board
Masking tape

Craft knife
Tape measure or ruler
Satinwood paint in stencil color
Artists' paintbrush
Matt polyurethane varnish
Varnish brush

TIPS
- For a stippled paint effect, use a stencil brush.
- To make the floor resemble a painted floor cloth, paint a separate border design around the edges of the room.

PATTERN & FORM

"When I'm throwing a plate I do think,
Oh, this'll be a lark to decorate"

Quentin Bell, English ceramicist

LEFT Even the esteemed designer Charles Eames had his light-hearted moments, such as when he designed this Hang It All rack, with its large, multi-colored gob-stopper hanging hooks.

In the '50s certain patterns and forms recurred again and again. The obsessions for surface pattern design included anything atomic, scientific, fantastic, foreign, or graphic. In terms of shape, it was a mixture of organic forms modernized to suit the "contemporary decade" and the appliance of science on everyday objects in the home. These influences affected everything from furniture shapes to food packaging. In many cases, designers combined these obsessions, for example, molecular motifs placed on a graphic background.

ABOVE Far too good for everyday trash, this vintage waste paper bin is a visual catalogue of '50s' vases, and flowers positioned on colored shapes, just like many fabric designs of the day.

LEFT In the '50s, clocks took the shape of television sets and other inventions. This modern version picks up on the theme.

The atomic age

In the '50s, such was the excitement attached to the many scientific breakthroughs that it seemed as if atoms were being split and rockets blasted into space almost on a daily basis. Consequently, anything atomic and space age spelled contemporary with a capital C. Science was the new buzzword and it inspired product and surface pattern designers everywhere.

One particularly influential body was the Festival Pattern Group, set up prior to the 1952 Festival of Britain. Its brief was to design patterns inspired by crystal structures for use throughout the festival. Cystallography (the newly developed scientific study of crystals and their structures) was the basis for the designs. The Pattern Group was briefed to provide scientific, abstract and natural designs in a fresh modern style for the new decade. The designs were to be used across a variety of media at the festival: furnishing fabrics, carpets and wallpapers, ceramics, glass, linoleum, plastic laminate, furniture, and lighting.

Invitations to participate in the group were sent to twenty-six manufacturers, such as Warners, Heals, Wedgwood, and Poole, rather than individual designers. The blueprint drawings were provided by a Cambridge scientist and included a variety of substances, such as insulin, hemoglobin and quartz, as well as new discoveries, such as polythene and polyvinyl chloride (PVC). As manufacturers were still restricted by postwar color rationing, the designers were limited to using a maximum of four colors and instructed to interpret the magnified, microscopic designs quite literally. The design source was often credited in the name of the final product, such as Harwell china, named after the British atomic reactor.

Atomic patterns can be identified by their spindly cotton bud-like symbols, graphic designs, amoeba-like asymmetric shapes, complex interlocking linear marks and rounded ends (the latter was a phenomenon that rapidly became known as the cocktail cherry look). Colors are usually in the modern color palette. To create atomic patterns for a set of place mats, see pages 50–51.

ABOVE A modern version of a '50s classic: the atomic clock. There are larger cocktail cherries at the positions of 3, 6, 9, and 12 o'clock for easy time-keeping.

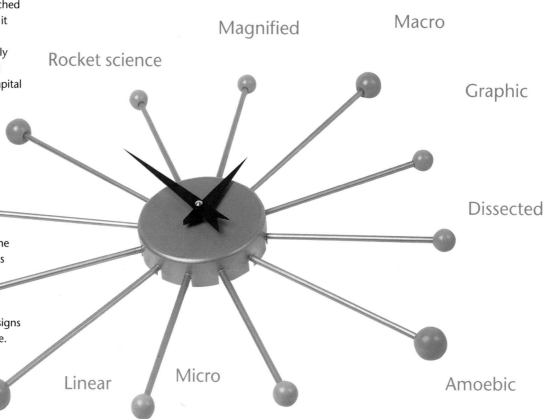

Rocket science

Magnified

Macro

Graphic

Dissected

Amoebic

Micro

Linear

Microscopic

Home thoughts from abroad

As incomes rose and air travel became more commonplace, Europe opened up for tourism. As a result, whimsical patterns inspired by foreign climes became a preoccupation on everything from dress fabrics to ceramics.

Paris was a favorite destination for the British because of its combination of sophistication and romance. The passion for France and Paris in particular is seen in the popularity of poodle motifs, artists' palettes, street cafe designs, and market scenes. This obsession with light-hearted and escapist patterns was a reaction against the grinding realism of the '30s and '40s and lasted well into the decade.

Other more exotic designs featuring nubile dancers or people in ethnic costume, abounded. Usually stereotypes, but never overtly racial, the people featured always seemed happy and content with their lot. These designs were probably meant to be a positive, tropical antidote to the Cold War hanging over Europe and America. The '50s' passion for stereotyping domestic roles and happy families meant that whatever the product—whether a sweet dish, decorative wall plaque, or oversized lamp base—there was always a matching partner. As Mark Burns, an American collector of '50s kitsch, comments in his book *50s Homestyle*:

"For every boy there had to be a girl—no matter how sexually ambiguous the boy. Mrs. Housewife certainly had no problem choosing happy couples of any ethnic flavor . . . Matador and Matadorette, Nubian and Nubianette . . . everything was smothered with overtones of the contented and complementary twosome."

Another motif common to the '50s was the boomerang, as it exemplified the allure of distant lands, plus it resembled a three-dimensional speeding jet-winged plane or the tail fin on a rocket. (Instructions for making a boomerang table are on pages 80–81.)

ABOVE Typifying the obsession with all things French, this cheese platter would have been the height of sophistication at a dinner party.

LEFT Foreign girls pictured on '50s decorative objects were invariably dancing and always sultry and exotic. Many of these plates were asymmetrical and intended for display on the wall.

Graphic organic

"One arrives at simplicity ... as one approaches the real meaning of things."

*Constantin Brancusi,
Romanian sculptor*

Although graphic and organic seem like two polar themes, in the '50s they were closely connected. In terms of product shape, the forms may be gentle and organic, with voluptuous curves being commonplace. However, for pattern design, it seemed that even Mother Nature became modern. Fruits and birds often appeared as dissected or X-ray images, with graphic cross-sections replacing more traditional painterly styles. Often these natural images became far removed from their original source material and adopted a graphic impact due to the nonnatural colors used and the magnified scale. Leaves and flowers became simplified, skeletal, and elongated. These spidery images were often shown on a similarly "scratched" background.

Apart from science, the other major influence was modern art. Sculptors such as Henry Moore, Barbara Hepworth, and Constantin Brancusi were creating simple, clean forms and the work of artists like Paul Klee, Wassily Kandinsky, and Joan Miro commonly featured strong colors and graphic shapes to give a striking visual impression. Another artist,

LEFT Scratched lines and amoebic-type blobs are common to many '50s pattern designs. This fabric is unusual for the dense patterning, creating a very busy design.

Alexander Calder, is most famous for his airy mobiles featuring asymmetrical metal shapes attached to a wire structure. As abstract designs replaced more literal work, stark line-drawn motifs were often superimposed on irregular blob-like shapes. This "framing" gave the motifs an importance and many of the designs resembled miniature icons, each displayed within an individual altar.

SGRAFFITO

This is a complex decorative ceramic technique in which a layer of glaze is applied, then scratched or combed away to reveal the base color. Today, sgraffito is most usually executed in a dark-chocolate, black, or navy-blue glaze to offer maximum contrast against the exposed areas.

Sgraffito ceramics (and occasionally glassware) fit well into any retro interior. They can either appear starkly modern or equally at ease with studio pottery depending on how the pattern has been executed.

RIGHT Contemporary ceramics with sgraffito designs. The patterns look particularly effective when done in black and white, or cream, as this gives the maximum contrast.

Scratched

Geometric

Abstract

Biomorphic

Linear

Packaging

Alongside the mightier, world-shattering events of the decade, such as the splitting of the atom, the average person will probably be far more interested in the fact that sliced bread was launched on an unsuspecting public in 1953 with the snappy slogan "sliced and wrapped for cleanliness." Other defining moments included the end of sweet rationing in 1953, the increased availability of ready meals and frozen foods, and the changing technology allowing plastics and PVC wrap (plastic wrap) to be used for packaging.

The list of product launches runs like a supermarket cart dash, with self-service supermarkets themselves being introduced in 1951. This change in shopping habits meant that product packaging had to change. Some items traditionally sold loose, such as flour, confectionery, and biscuits, were packaged for the first time. All products had to stand out from competitors' brands on the shelves. Packages became simpler in design with an emphasis on a brand name or logo for easy recognition. Graphics superseded images as they enticed customers with the promise of added value, easy-to-follow instructions and the latest innovations.

In the United States, some manufacturers used the opportunity to build brand awareness by making the product packaging reusable. Some of the most common items to be used were glasses with silk-screened patterns in varying designs. This encouraged the customer to collect the whole series, thus building brand loyalty. Once the glasses were empty, they were ideal as juice or milk glasses. This concept was pioneered by Kraft Foods who called the free glasses "swanky swigs". Another classic is the "Howdy Doody" glass from 1953, originally sold filled with peanut butter—generations of Americans were brought up drinking their milk from Howdy Doody glasses, anxious to finish the drink to see which character was at the bottom of the glass.

Today, for a retro look at mealtimes, buy china or juice glasses with silk-screen printed patterns in bright, bold designs. Or customize standard tumblers by painting with specialist glass paint from art shops. For an authentic '50s feel, choose non-translucent paints and keep to simple designs such as polka dots, cheery daisies or classic diner style slogans such as "special today" or "guaranteed ice cold".

Due to the throwaway nature of packaging, it is unlikely that you have any original samples from the '50s. Unless, of course, you are as forward-thinking as collector Robert Opie, who has amassed a collection of over 300,000 advertisements and packets dating from the past century—enough for him to open a museum and still have plenty left over. Be warned, it started from a single chocolate bar wrapper that he decided not to throw away!

BRINGING THE LOOK TO YOUR KITCHEN

The best way to give a corner of your kitchen a retro fix is to take a close look around the local supermarket and pick out classic brands which have changed little since the '50s. Prime contenders include baked beans, tinned soup, California raisins, custard powder, marmalade or labels on fruit crates. If you want to eat your art first, take the labels or empty boxes down to your local copy shop and have them laminated as placemats. Either use varying designs for different meal times, such as cereal packets or marmalades for breakfasts, or have a gastronomic medley by concentrating on color rather than brand.

If you have open shelves in the kitchen, keep the best of today's packaging on display rather than behind closed doors. Rather than cramming everything onto a shelf, display related items in small groups. Even economy baked beans will look stylish if you stack a number of the same design together and display with a flourish rather than an apology. Alternatively, pile a pyramid of tins of a single design on a window sill for maximum graphic effect.

Packaging can also inspire designs for painted canvasses. Look especially at the bold and

striking designs of '50s washing powder packets and the bubbles, flashes and stripes as inspiration. Using pre-stretched canvases, paint with water-based paints and hang in the kitchen for your own art supermarket. Another option is to use the simpler designs for frosting onto glass. (Instructions for frosting are on page 137.)

LEFT Modern ceramics with witty graphic designs are typical of today's fascination with typefaces and computer-style icons on everyday objects such as spelling out the obvious by saying "hot" or "water" or "drink me."

ABOVE Some of the most striking graphic designs from the '50s have come from washing powder packaging. As washing machines became commonplace in homes, the number of brands of powder multiplied rapidly. Their boldness and sheer gusto are wonderful—all promising the whitest, brightest, soapiest wash.

SPACE AGE PLACEMATS

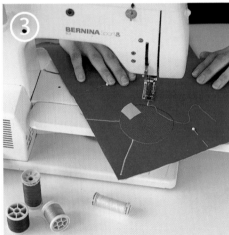

Go back to the future with these space-age placemats—excellent for persuading would-be astronauts to eat their meals!

1. Sketch the designs on paper, keeping them bold and simple. Pin one rectangle of the plain cotton to the Vilene.

2. Following the manufacturer's instructions, iron the Bondaweb onto the wrong side of the fabric scraps, protecting the iron from the hemming tape by placing an old tea towel over the fabrics. Referring to the sketch, draw the spaceship shapes on the paper of the Bondawebbed fabric and cut out the shapes.

3. Iron the taped shapes onto the right side of the placemat. Using matching thread and satin stitch, machine-stitch around the edges of the appliquéd motifs to secure them. Draw on details with the vanishing marker pen and stitch. Iron.

4. Place another rectangle on top of the embroidered placemat and pin. Using straight stitch, sew around the edge, leaving a 6in. opening along one narrow side. Trim off excess fabric and Vilene at the corners and turn to the right side. Iron. Fold in and pin the opening. Top stitch around the edge of the placemat ¹⁄₄in. from the edge, closing the opening as you go.

YOU WILL NEED (for 4 placemats)
Paper and pencil
1³⁄₈yd of plain cotton fabric 45in. wide, cut into eight pieces each 12 × 18in.
1yd heavy sew-in Vilene, cut into four pieces each 12 × 18in.
Pins
Iron
¹⁄₂yd hemming tape

Scraps of plain cotton in bright colors and threads to match
Old tea towel
Scissors
Matching thread
Sewing machine
Vanishing quilt marker pen

TIPS
- Keep the design to the corners or edges of the mats as the center will be hidden by the china.
- Stitch a different design on each placemat—think of designs inspired by atoms, spaceships or aliens! Look at children's comics for ideas.
- For a thicker placemat, add a layer of cotton batting or Vilene Compressed Volume Fleece below the top fabric.

FABRICS

"Americans embraced modernity as a new gospel and rushed to deck out their homes with curtains broadcasting icons of innovation: images of atoms, cell structures, automobiles, satellites and television sets."

Gideon Bosker, American physician

With a single fabric, the various elements of a room—color, pattern, comfort, and texture—can be brought together. In a retro interior, fabric can be the basis for setting the tone of the room, whether folksy, modern, witty, or tactile. A textile design can be the foundation for the whole color scheme. Alternatively, it can introduce an element of wit in an otherwise serious interior, or provide the raw materials for a selection of easy-to-make accessories such as cushions, bed linens, and table linens, bringing character to a room for very little expense.

In the '50s, textile designs were usually printed onto cotton, linen, or the new range of synthetic fabrics. Bark cloth is a term frequently used to describe '50s fabrics—this was a generic term given to a two-ply woven

LEFT A vintage linen cabinet piled high with crisp cottons and cozy winceyette.

cotton with a nubby texture, rather like tree bark. Today, most homes concentrate on using natural fibers in the home, and synthetic fabrics are used more widely in corporate environments where performance or longevity are necessary.

The general mood for contemporary interiors is to use fabrics in a simpler, less fussy way. Window treatments are pared down, and the frills and swags of the '80s are thankfully confined to the trashcan as a simpler style prevails. However, this does not mean that fabric is a no-go area; it just needs a little consideration. It is far easier to give a new look to a room by replacing curtains, cushions, and bed linens than starting again with new furniture. This chapter concerns itself with the printed designs common in the '50s. Woven fabrics were also used, particularly for upholstery, but it is the prints of the '50s that can give a room instant retro style.

ABOVE A modern sofa is given the retro treatment with slip covers in a '50s-style "bracken" fabric. Together with the plywood chair and plenty of wood and light, this living room is an excellent mix of retro and modern styles.

Flower power

Long before the "flower power" term was coined for '60s fashions and attitudes, many '50s homes were covered in blooms. Of all fabric designs popular in this decade, florals have stood the test of time. Today flower motifs continue to sell extraordinarily well. Although designers, trend stylists, and some retailers may snobbishy declare at intervals that floral is dead and that our homes should be furnished in plain fabrics, the public continues to demand floral fabric designs as they provide a comfortable, easy-to-live-with home environment..

However, this is not to say that all floral fabrics around today are good designs. So in looking for retro florals, be prepared to prune away the "deadwood" designs in search of fun, fresh interpretations. Colors should be clear rather than muddy, even if it is a pastel colorway. Fifties florals are generally simply drawn, whether in a simplified or painterly style. Big blowsy designs are as common as smaller posy-type motifs, and for a real '50s feel are often combined with a patterned background, such a dot, stripe, or check. At the beginning of the decade, manufacturers were limited to printing with only four to six colors, so stick with designs that have fewer colors (check the fabric selvage where each individual color will be shown), rather than elaborate botanical renderings that will sometimes have up to twenty different colors.

LEFT AND RIGHT Swatches of modern and vintage cheery floral fabrics, characterized by their clear colors and bold designs.

For a guaranteed retro feel, choose floral fabrics containing any of the following colors—duck-egg blue, soft-leaf green, butter yellow, powder pink, apple green, and off-white. Many fabric manufacturers today include such colorways within their collections whether they are original patterns from the '50s being reissued, or from young designers leaving college. Don't be worried about combining different patterns or scales. To ensure that the mix of designs works, follow these simple guidelines: Stick to one type of flower (for example roses) in different sizes or styles; have a key color (such as raspberry) which is picked up in all the fabrics; choose just two floral fabrics and liven them up with two-color woven stripes or checks; and finally, keep the decoration of the floors, walls, and furniture very simple to provide a foil for the busy patterns.

Conversational prints

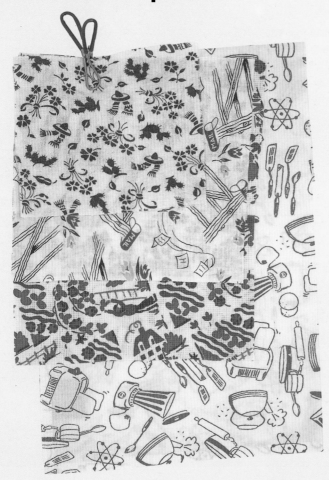

The term *conversational print* is little known outside the design world. It is a themed or story print that is not classifiable under another heading such as floral or geometric. As such, it includes a wide range of whimsical and fantastic designs. These fabrics were extremely popular in the '50s, and appeared on fabrics for both fashion and furnishing. In fact the two types of fabrics were often interchangeable—printed cottons were just as likely to be used for kitchen curtains as for

aprons, and heavier-weight full-length curtains were commonly recycled into clothing.

Although conversationals appeared in both Britain and the United States, American designs seem to illustrate a greater range of ideas. Certain images crop up again and again—stereotypes of foreign or exotic people drawn in a rather naive manner. Mexican and Chinese people regularly appear with typical props—sombreros and cacti, coolie hats,

pagodas, and paper lanterns. Certain cities and lifestyles were seen as exotic or sophisticated, the most common being Paris and the French Riviera. Closer to home, patterns harked back to a more rural lifestyle and "the good old days"—pioneer caravans; wigwams; or fertile, abundant fields. Everyday objects such as mailboxes were immortalized. Another preoccupation was food and that great American tradition, diners. Finally, anything to do with fantasy or children's

make-believe appeared with regularity—cowboys and pirates jostle for space with ballet dancers and circus acts. It seems that anything goes with conversationals—if it could be drawn, it was printed.

Fewer novelty prints are produced today so the only designs available may be vintage fabrics in small-size pieces. Even if the swatches are small, don't throw them away, but preserve them in a '50s wall quilt as a

potpourri collection of the designs of the times. Either sew using a simple patchwork block design, combined with plenty of calico to offset the busy patterns. Alternatively, for a more contemporary look, create an instant no-sew wall hanging (see pages 64–65 for details). Other sources for novelty prints are the many companies producing cotton fabrics for the quilt market. They prove that the market for conversationals is as lively today as fifty years ago.

ABOVE Vintage and modern conversational prints. Some of the old designs are printed on feedsack cotton. This fabric was sewn into bags containing flour and animal feed. When the bags were empty, the seams were carefully unpicked and the cotton laundered and converted into clothing or quilts. This practice started during the Depression and continued well into the '50s.

Ginghams, checks, and stripes

What is it about ginghams and retro—the two seem to go hand in hand? Is it a reminder of childhood—school dresses, first needlework smocking projects, Grandma's bathroom curtains? Even if we are not children of the '50s, there is something essentially nostalgic and familiar about these simple two-color woven checked fabrics.

Ginghams are traditionally pure cotton with an equal number of dyed and bleached threads across the warp and weft of the fabric to give the even check. Traditional ginghams have a double thread at the edge of each check which gives a raised effect in the weave. Although the term *gingham* comes from the Malay word *gingan*, the majority of ginghams today are woven in China. For such a finely woven fabric, it is remarkably inexpensive, and is available in a number of colorways, including tomato red, orange, yellow, black, lilac, and a variety of shades of blue and green.

Because of the small scale of the pattern, this dress-weight fabric makes wonderful cafe curtains in a kitchen or bathroom and is excellent in a nursery. It can also be used as generous, floor-length curtains with a simple tab top or ties, combined with a Roman blind in a more substantial fabric to block the light. The trick is not to skimp on the fabric—gingham is one of the cheapest fabrics available so make sure you use a sufficient amount, even if the heading style is simple. To help gingham curtains hang properly, sew with a curtain lining to give weight or insert metal curtain-weight tape in the hems. Blue-and-white gingham was also used traditionally for chair covers on furniture when not in use. Use it today as slipcovers to jazz up small slipper chairs, or for a motley selection of chairs around a dining table. As gingham is a dress fabric, it does not have to pass the necessary fire retardancy regulations, so always use with a fire retardant liner. This is also essential to give weight and increased durability.

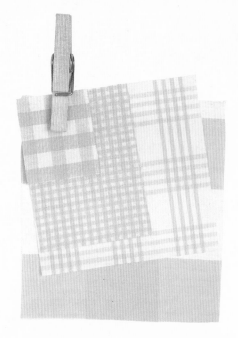

With the typical '50s zest for "more is better," ginghams are often combined with florals or other checks and stripes for an authentic retro feel. Heavier woven cottons (not strictly ginghams, but a subtle two-color version of a madras check) make ideal loose covers for upholstery. Junk-shop chairs can be given a new lease on life with a coat of paint and a recovered seat in a madras check. For variety, paint chairs in the same color, but change the fabric on the seats. Ginghams and other woven checks are excellent for table linen—try bordering a floral tablecloth with a checked border, for example.

LEFT AND ABOVE A variety of ginghams and madras cottons. Although the fabrics only contain two colors, when combined together they are remarkably lively because of their varying scale.

RIGHT Typical scrap quilt using cotton fabrics from the '40s and '50s. In the spirit of "waste not, want not," one-patch designs such as this clamshell can utilize even the smallest of scraps.

Modern geometrics

As befits the "contemporary" decade, modern geometric patterns were extremely popular during the '50s. There were several influences for this trend. Many textile designers were inspired by the modern art produced by artists and sculptors such as Picasso, Miro, Braque, and Brancusi. Their stark, simple, graphic styles were easy to interpret and print as fabric designs, and the limitation on the number of print colors makes the images appear even bolder. David Whitehead, one of the leading manufacturers of the decade, commissioned striking designs from a number of young designers and artists such as Henry Moore and Eduardo Paolozzi. Today Whitehead textiles are extremely collectible and include contemporary designs by Marion Mahler,

Jacqueline Groag, and Terence Conran, printed onto cotton and rayon.

Large-scale patterns complemented the less fussy furniture of the '50s, whether home owners furnished their homes in the simple Scandinavian style or the overtly modern mood. Contemporary fabric patterns were favored by Scandinavians, in particular the trend-setting designs of Astrid Sampe and Nordiska Kompaniet, the textile company where she was head of design from 1937 for thirty-four years. Today, Swedish and Finnish companies such as IKEA, Boras, Mairo, and Marimekko continue to lead the way in bold geometrics, with furnishing fabrics, bed linens, and accessories available worldwide.

The enthusiasm for large abstract or geometric designs was also influenced by house styles. In Britain and the United States, architects were designing postwar homes with large picture windows, rather than the small, fussier, multi-paned windows of previous decades. These modern fabric designs were ideal for such a large expanse of glass, and provided a dramatic accent in an otherwise simply furnished room. However, the flip side to this bold modernity was that in some interiors the "more is better" school of thought prevailed, resulting in rooms that were best viewed through dark glasses. Bold patterned curtains fought stylewise with unsubtle carpet designs, dramatic ceramics, and quirky or downright kitsch accessories and lighting. Unfortunately,

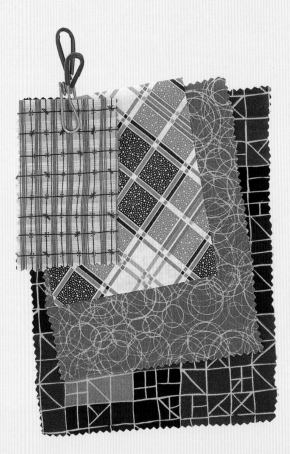

it is this image of chaotic non-coordination that has often branded the decade as an era of excessive taste.

With a little thought, such bold designs can be incorporated with style into a retro scheme today, without being too overpowering. One idea is to let the fabric dictate the color scheme of the whole room. Any window treatments in modern geometrics should be kept simple—as further decoration is unnecessary for such bold designs. Upholstery fabrics or bed linen should be plain so as not to conflict with the main fabric design. For added interest, think about contrasting textures, such as a sofa covered in a cord, velvet, or brushed cotton; gun-tufted wool

rugs in one color but with a sculpted surface or throws with interesting weaves. Use fabric designs in the same colors as the main print but of a much smaller scale for cushions. Look at the swatches above for ideas on combinations.

Any accessories should be plain and graphic—consider bold sgraffito ceramics or colored glass vases with a single bloom. Decorative schemes must be kept simple—if you lean toward the hoarder style of decorating rather than minimalism, try to hide or disguise the majority of your possessions with smart storage, to avoid detracting from the boldness of the soft furnishings. Alternatively, let these art-inspired fabrics become pieces of art. Using

artists' canvas, stretch a length of fabric tightly around the board and staple in place. Either hang or casually prop against the wall for a modern-art gallery feel. For even more impact, make up several canvases in different designs (but with a color scheme for unity) such as the blue and white fabrics shown opposite, or use one fabric divided over three or four canvases to accentuate a geometric pattern. This is a good way of displaying original '50s fabrics, which you might find, as they may be in short lengths unsuitable for making into curtains.

ABOVE Typical geometric patterns of the '50s and contemporary equivalents happily coordinate when careful thought is given to color combinations.

LUCIENNE DAY (B.1917)

"I'm a practical person. I wanted what I was doing to be useful to people."

The most well-known fabric of the decade was by British textile designer, Lucienne Day. Called Calyx, this striking abstract design of cone shapes strung together like kite strings has become iconic as a '50s image. It is reminiscent of the mobiles of Alexander Calder and the work of artists Miro and Klee. It was produced in a number of daring colorways on linen fabric—lime green, turquoise, and white on black; and yellow, orange, and black on terra-cotta. The design was commissioned for use in one of the Festival of Britain's pavilions, by Heal's of London, a department store renowned for its contemporary design. Calyx

later won a gold medal at the Milan Triennale in 1951, and another design award from the American Institute of Decorators in 1952, the first time a non-American had won this accolade.

Although trained as a textile designer, Day's surface pattern designs were also successful when transposed onto other media such as carpets, ceramics, and laminated plastics. She worked as a freelance designer for a number of companies including Heal's, Sanderson, Liberty, and Edinburgh Weavers in Britain and Rosenthal China and Rasch Wallpapers in Germany. Like Calyx, her other textile designs, such as Miscellany, Tickertape, Linear, Spectator, and Graphica were equally graphic.

Like many textiles designed for the domestic market, Day was limited to using a few colors—in retrospect, this probably gives the designs greater dramatic impact. They are characterized by blobs of color often in a linear format, overprinted with grids, lines, dots, or textured, scratched effects. Entirely abstract, they make reference to the atomic images or skeletal leaf forms so popular at the time. Urban in appeal, they were just right for the large picture windows that were popular in new house designs and large public spaces. Today, Day's textiles are much sought after and command premium prices.

After several decades working on one-off wall hangings, Day is back at the forefront of the design world. The Habitat stores have commissioned one of her '50s designs, Leaf, for use as bed linen, a new departure for her as duvet covers were not even invented at the time of its launch. It shows how her timeless designs can be appreciated by a new generation and easily be incorporated into today's interiors.

LEFT Graphica, by Lucienne Day, was originally sold as a fabric in 1954, and later modified into a wallpaper. The design is available again and looks just as fresh half a century later.

THIS PAGE Leaf, also by Lucienne Day, was originally designed in the '50s, and was relaunched in 1999 by Habitat. The bold and graphic design is complemented in this bedroom by a sculptural lamp and simple accessories

PATTERN

NO-SEW WALL HANGING

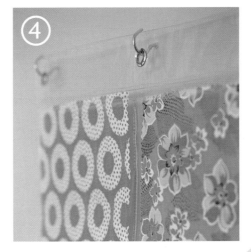

This easy-to-make wall hanging provides an ideal way to display vintage fabrics.

1. Lay fabrics out in the order you wish to place them in the pockets trying to balance colors and dominant patterns. Keeping the designs in the correct placement order, remove and iron the fabrics.

2. Using pinking shears, cut the fabrics into 4 × 6in. rectangles (you may find it easier to cut out a cardboard template to ensure all pieces are the same size).

3. Place in the plastic pockets from the reverse side (i.e. so the openings will be next to the wall when hung).

4. Using a pencil, mark the position of the hooks on the wall. Drill holes, insert the rawl plugs, and screw in the cup hooks. Hang the plastic holder.

YOU WILL NEED

Selection of vintage cotton fabrics
Plastic 24-pocket CD/photo holder (each pocket 4 × 6in.)
Iron
Pinking shears
Pencil
Wood drill

Metal cup hooks (quantity depends on the number of riveted holes in the plastic holder)
Rawl plugs

TIPS

- It is a good idea to leave the arrangement of fabrics to one side and go back to it after a while to look at it with a fresh eye. Any rearrangement necessary to achieve a better balance will then be more obvious.
- To ensure the plastic holder hangs straight, open it up and flatten under heavy books for a few days before using it. As the fabric has no weight, the hanging can be made to hang taut by hammering two picture pins into the bottom corners.
- Instead of vintage fabrics, you could use old packaging or postcards in the pockets. Repeat the same image for a "Warhol" effect.
- To prevent the fabrics fading, do not hang in direct sunlight.

FURNITURE

"The concept of organic design stems from living organisms
. . . an ideal in organic design was the concept of a single
harmonious unit of one-piece construction."

Cherie and Kenneth Fehrman, Postwar Interior Design

Going retro on furniture is like taking a whistle-stop global tour. The decade was bursting with creativity with furniture designs coming from product designers, architects, and sculptors. Combined with manufacturing and technological advances made in the '40s, furniture of the '50s could be modern, yet human in scale and comfort, or homely, witty, or luxurious. Many designs are still made, and some of the designers have become living legends of this century.

There were four main areas of furniture design in the '50s, each with their signature look—American modern, Scandinavian contemporary, British post-utility, and Italian designer. The subtle differences are apparent in the availability of materials, the ease with

LEFT Walls of glass, bold color, and a sculptural wire Bertoia chair add up to a contemporary retro style.

which consumers accepted and bought the new designs, and finally historical traditions. Today, irrespective of the country of origin, the designs are available globally either as period originals or as contemporary versions.

THE NEW LOOK—ORGANIC, ASYMMETRIC, ERGONOMIC

For furniture, the '50s was a decade with a new attitude. Many designers threw out the rule book and embraced new ideas. The two key features of good '50s designs were organic and asymmetric forms and ergonomic functionality. The desire for natural shapes was widely influenced by sculptors such as Constantin Brancusi, a Romanian who specialized in gently undulating abstract shapes, and Alexander Calder, an American artist whose delicate asymmetric metal "blob" mobiles were extremely popular. The organic

phenomenon had been gaining popularity since the '40s when the Museum of Modern Art (MOMA) in New York, staged a competition for organic design. Gently rounded designs were all the rage and asymmetry was particularly prevalent. Many designs by the famous four in furniture—Charles Eames, Robin Day, Arne Jacobsen, and Eero Saarinen—can be called organic.

Ergonomic design is something now taken for granted, but in the '50s it was quite revolutionary. It resulted in furniture, particularly chair designs, that fitted the body and was comfortable. Unlike the stark Modernist designs of the '30s, which also espoused fitness for purpose in their saying "form follows function," designs from the '50s look gentler.

Despite these common philosophies, innovative furniture designs gained acceptance at different speeds on either side of the Atlantic mainly due to economic prosperity of the countries concerned, but also to an extent due to Britain's slow-changing traditional values.

At the beginning of the decade rationing was still in force in Britain in the form of the Utility Furniture scheme. This program, which lasted until 1952, severely limited the choice of furniture available and designs were characterized by their rectilinear and undecorated forms, based mainly on Modernist furniture and arts-and-crafts ideals. Only "bombees" (people whose houses had been bombed) and newlyweds were allowed to buy new Utility furniture. Everyone else had to make do with secondhand items.

Another lesser known objective of Utility was to re-educate the public on what was

considered to be good design. This was tackled by a government-funded organization, The Council of Industrial Design, using wartime propaganda tactics to promote the message on a massive scale. Prewar furniture had not evolved much from turn-of-the-century designs—overstuffed, oversized upholstery in drab fabrics, often with fussy decoration such as antimacassars. Dark, heavily varnished woods such as mahogany were favored for dining furniture, and kitchens were a throwback to pre-World War I designs when domestic help was commonplace.

THE NEW DESIGNERS

The '50s brought a breath of fresh air. At public exhibitions such as the Festival of Britain, young furniture designers were

encouraged to exhibit or to manufacture new, modern designs. The Antelope chairs by Ernest Race (1913–1964) are typical of this new look—spindly steel frames supported seats in brightly colored plywood. The chairs were commissioned in the hundreds for the Brighton Pavilion. A practical feature was the white ball feet, designed to stop chair legs sinking into the grass. These can be seen as the precursors to the "cocktail cherry" fad for rounded ends combined with apparently insubstantial frames.

Race was determined to break the mold of traditional manufacturers who wanted to produce, in his words, "the same old stuff, bulky, ostentatious, over ornamented and apparently polished by the process used for making toffee apples" (from Madeleine Marsh, *Collecting The 1950s*). Despite its fresh look, the Antelope range was not aggressively modern. In essence, it was a traditional Windsor chair design, brought up to date with modern materials. Race's approach was vindicated as the range won a silver medal at the prestigious design exhibition, the Milan Triennale in 1954.

Robin Day (b.1915) was another forward-looking designer, keen to break the mold of traditional design. Working closely with

manufacturer Hille, he produced a series of innovative molded plywood chairs, sleek sofa beds, upholstery, and functional low-cost storage. His work first gained international recognition when, with Clive Latimer, he won first prize in a low cost furniture design competition at New York's Museum of Modern Art. Their elegant storage unit was unlike anything seen before in Britain—a light wood cabinet with gently curved edges that seemed to float mid-air, supported by only two slender metal rod legs, which were attached to the wall. Despite the plaudits, the cabinet was never put into production, much to the dismay of the designers.

Although there was a wariness from the older generation, such furniture, quickly dubbed the "contemporary style," was like manna from heaven to a young, design-aware public, who wanted to set up home in a modern style different from that of their parents. G-Plan was a major British manufacturer, producing designs in light woods, such as plywood, beech, and elm. This modular furniture was designed to give flexible interior space. These add-on designs also helped young couples gradually to buy a cohesive collection of furniture for their homes.

LEFT The Tulip chair and table by Eero Saarinen are made from fiberglass and aluminium.

ABOVE Robin Day's classic Polyprop chair has recently been put back into production, confirming its longlasting popularity

RIGHT Another Robin Day design. The simple lines provide a calm diversion against the more lively wall paper.

CHARLES EAMES (1907–1978)

"Recognizing the need is the primary condition for design."

Unarguably one of the seminal designers of the '50s, Charles Eames and his wife, Ray (1912–1988), became, along with their furniture, icons of the decade. After studying architecture, Eames opened his own design office in 1930. However, in 1936, he accepted a fellowship at Cranbrook Academy of Arts, Michigan, and became head of the experimental design department a year later.

Eames's recognition and success began in 1940 when, in collaboration with Eero Saarinen, he designed the prizewinning plywood Relaxation chair, for a competition at MOMA in New York. Further exhibitions of his work at MOMA followed throughout the '40s. One of Eames's guiding principles was to use and manipulate the seat forms to fit the human body, without the need for cushioned upholstery. So although his designs seemed avant-garde at the time, because of their shapes and use of unusual materials, they were always well received because they fulfilled the basic criteria of comfort and fitness for purpose.

Having always considered the seat and the leg supports of a chair to be separate elements and therefore not necessarily made of the same substance, Eames had often combined different materials in his revolutionary designs. Early work combined plywood for seats and elegant steel rod for legs. In the '50s, Eames's designs became less organic as he introduced other materials into his work. As a result of working closely with Zenith Plastics, Eames understood the possibilities of resin-impregnated fiberglass. The result was his range of DAR chairs, which went into mass production in 1951.

The molded one-piece seat-shell came in a choice of nine bright colors such as lemon yellow, seafoam green, mustard, and red, and injected a shot of fun to his otherwise elegant repertoire. The chairs are supported on struts of steel rod in several design variations—the Eiffel Tower base, the cat's cradle base, and the rocker that looks rather like the landing skis of a seaplane. Eames believed that well-designed furniture should be affordable and the DAR chair was produced and sold by the Herman Miller furniture company for thirty-five dollars, about half the price of conventionally constructed chairs. Still in production, the DAR chair has been much imitated by other manufacturers.

Eames was full of innovative ideas, a typical example being his sofa compact of 1954. A streamlined and elegant design, it was one of the first sofas to arrive flat-packed for home assembly by the customer. His designs became more substantial as the decade progressed and his most sumptuous design (and interestingly, the one with least commercial success) has to be the 670 lounger chair and ottoman of 1956. Made of a molded plywood frame with a rosewood veneer, it was upholstered in leather. Thoroughly masculine in design, it embodied complete relaxation and luxury.

Eames was more than just a furniture designer. He recognized that communication and information were as key to postwar America as design and manufacturing. Together the Eameses worked on other projects including exhibition design, books, and film production. Through these other media, which varied from small-scale entertainments for friends and colleagues to productions for corporate business and the government, Charles and Ray Eames were elevated to the height of cultural ambassadors of the '50s. Such educational activities continue today, organized by the Eameses' daughter.

LEFT Eames designed various options for his DAR chair frame. This one clearly shows the Eiffel Tower base.

Wood-framed upholstery designed by Lucien Ercolani for his company Ercol was typical of the new lightweight furniture. Like Race's Antelope chair, it was based on traditional Windsor shapes. These designs were driven by practicality as well as aesthetics as timber was in short supply and Ercolani's new-look furniture required less raw materials. Ercol furniture inspired several Scandinavian designers to produce similar models, and proved equally popular with homemakers as the slender designs were visually space enhancing.

One criticism leveled at British design is that many manufacturers simply tried to put a '50s veneer onto traditional pieces, such as the three-piece suite and sideboard, instead of

BELOW Noguchi's glass-topped, asymmetric table is both sculptural and practical.

RIGHT The Butterfly chair was actually designed by a team of designers, including Hardoy, in 1938, but became popular in the '50s as it was extremely inexpensive. Based on a campaign chair, it is a true chameleon, available with a vast range of covers from plan canvas to mock cow hide.

radically rethinking what kind of furniture was suitable for the new living spaces and lifestyles (by 1958 ten million people in Britain were living in postwar homes). In the United States for example, designers such as Charles Eames were creating tall, freestanding storage units, which also functioned as room dividers in the opened-up spaces. Others experimented with modular seating for maximum flexibility.

There were two prevailing popular styles for modern interiors in the United States—Scandinavian contemporary, typified by the work of Charles Eames for Knoll, and a sleek modern look using metal and the latest plastic technology. The major players in furniture manufacturing—Knoll International, Herman Miller, and Heywood Wakefield—were all keen to develop new collections and actively commissioned furniture designers, architects, and sculptors to create this new look. These manufacturers are still in existence today, developing exciting new designs, as well as continuing to manufacture '50s classics.

FURNITURE OF THE '50S

So what are the essential elements of '50s furniture? The following list refers to furniture

of this decade but could equally be used as a must-have list when shopping for contemporary designs. If the furniture meets the majority of the criteria, it's sure to fit happily into a retro-style home as it has the same spirit.

- an elegant simplicity of line, with a feeling of lightness, often due to the legginess of designs

- the use of lighter woods, complemented by vivid colors for upholstery

- comfort and practicality (the exception being Bertoia's wire chairs)

- the ingenious use of new materials such as fiberglass, plywood, chipboard, and hardboard, and designs that enabled furniture to be mass-produced or "flat packed"

- an unwillingness to simply reproduce past styles and therefore an attempt to experiment with new ideas and modern designs. Sometimes this resulted in exuberant, playful designs bordering on kitsch, but at least the effort was made not to simply rehash the work of previous decades.

Look at the list on the right for key furniture designers of the '50s. In all cases, their designs are still available today, and their ground-breaking furniture has inspired many copycat designs. However, it doesn't really matter whether you buy an original piece or an imitation as long as the piece is true to '50s styles and ideals.

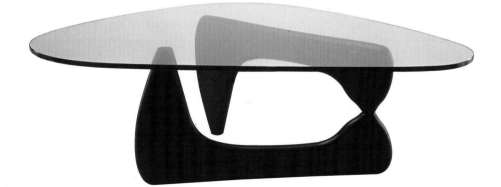

Alvar Aalto, Finland

Harry Bertoia, U.S.

Robin Day, England

Charles Eames, U.S.

Lucien Ercolani, England

Jorge Ferrari Hardoy,
  Argentina

Juhl Finn, Denmark

E. Gomme G-Plan, England

Poul Henningsen, Denmark

Arne Jacobsen, Denmark

Poul Kjaerholm, Denmark

Florence Knoll, U.S.

Bruno Mathsson, Sweden

George Nelson, U.S.

Isamu Noguchi, U.S.

Verner Panton, Denmark

Gio Ponti, Italy

Ernest Race, England

Eero Saarinen, U.S.

Hans Wegner, Denmark

HARRY BERTOIA (1915–1978)

"The urge for good design is the same as the urge to go on living. The assumption is that somewhere, hidden, is a better way of doing things."

Born in Italy, Bertoia moved to the United States as a teenager. After concentrating on architecture and silversmithing at art school, he went on to study and teach metalwork and graphic art at Cranbrook Academy in Michigan. The academy was a hot bed of talent in the '50s—other students included Charles Eames, Eero Saarinen, and Florence Knoll.

Although he worked briefly with the Eameses on plywood furniture, the designs Bertoia is most famous for are his range of wire chairs designed from 1951 to 1953 for Knoll International. His design brief from Florence Knoll was very open:

"Work on your own. If you come up with a piece of furniture, so much the better."

Bertoia was given a small room in the factory in which to work. He described his time there as being "a very happy one, the more I stayed, the more pleasurable it became."

Bertoia's designs were made of steel wire mesh and metal rod, bent and twisted into rounded forms—the chairs were as sculptural as they were functional. As he explains: "The chairs are studies in space, form, and metal too. If you look at them, you will find that they are mostly made of air, just like sculpture. Space passes right through them."

However, when used on their own, these airy sculptures were rather uncomfortable to sit on, so were usually fully upholstered with removable covers. For those aesthetes willing to put artistic appreciation over comfort, another option was the "bikini" cover, which covered the seat alone. The "chicken wire" range (as it is sometimes referred to) includes a number of shapes: the diamond chair and ottoman, the long-necked bird chair, the bar

stool, the dining chair, and the miniature child's chair for wannabe culture vultures. The longevity of the design is demonstrated by the fact that the entire range is still in production for Knoll International and sold worldwide.

ABOVE Proof that Bertoia's designs can look equally at home in a kitchen or design studio.

RIGHT A bevy of Bertoia's wire chairs, evoking memories of Hollywood's glamorous past with their pouting lipstick-bright upholstery.

ARNE JACOBSEN (1902–1971)

Of all the furniture designs produced in the '50s, it is perhaps Jacobsen's colored beech plywood chairs, the Ant series, which are instantly recognizable even if their creator's name is not. In fact Jacobsen was Denmark's leading architect of the '50s, but like so many other designers of this period, he worked across many design disciplines. The chair designs look as fresh today as in 1952 when they were first manufactured by Fritz Hansen in Denmark. The classic Ant, 3101, with its sinuous form and three gently splayed chrome-plated legs originally appeared in black and was a winner of the Grand Prix at the 1957 Milan Triennale. Today it is still *the* chair to have and seems equally at home in a kitchen, loft apartment, or corporate office. Later a fourth leg was added and the color palette extended.

The 3101 has spawned a host of imitators of slightly varying shapes and colors which are now sold by retailers the world over under various names. The Ant achieved notoriety in 1963 when one of its copies was photographed with Christine Keeler at the height of the Profumo political scandal in Britain. The reason for the success of the Ant chair is simple—it is extremely comfortable and fun to live with. The curvature of the seat, made from a single piece of plywood, fits the body and gives a little when one leans back.

Design purists probably still choose classic white or natural beech for a '50s Scandinavian look, but there is also a whole rainbow of colors to choose from. For a fun retro look, pick sorbet pastels such as lilac, lemon yellow, mint, or melon, or be daring and modern with scarlet, slate blue, yellow, or black.

LEFT So elegant, so '50s, so now. Jacobsen's Swan and Egg chairs are as covetable today as they were half a century ago.

RIGHT An army of Ant chairs, looking bright and breezy and not at all like a staid design classic.

Jacobsen was not a one-chair wonder and his other designs from the late '50s are equally in demand today. The Egg and Swan chairs (1958) were originally designed for the Royal SAS hotel in Copenhagen. This really was the "Jacobsen" hotel—he not only designed the building, but also designed everything else from the interior, furniture, and light fixtures right down to the ashtrays. The Egg really does wrap around the sitter and cocoon him in its organic form, while the Swan is like a Matisse cutout with its elegant winglike arms. Both chairs used molded fiberglass shells on an aluminium pedestal base and were upholstered with foam padding and a solid color cloth upholstery or leather.

The fact that Jacobsen's designs are as comfortable and popular fifty years on is surely testament of the view held by one of his contemporaries, Swedish furniture designer, Carl Malmsten: "moderation lasts, extremism palls."

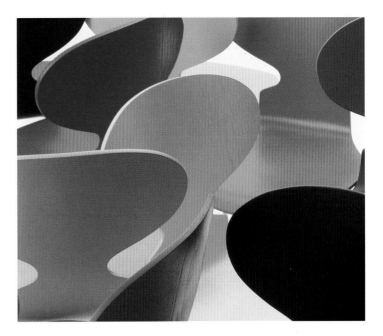

Fun and fabulous

"We are teased by the surreal description of chairs being 'occasional.' What are they when they are not being chairs?"

Mark Burns, collector of '50s kitsch

Not all furniture was simple, well-designed, and elegant. There was a large amount of quirky and downright kitsch furniture available, which was extremely popular. It cannot be ignored as a minority faction as there was a mainstream desire for novelty and fun. The '50s was the start of the home improvements boom. Several magazines were launched urging their readers, who were often young homeowners, to have a go at making small, jolly pieces of furniture, to paint or laminate in bright colors. Today, with the vast selection of products available , it's child's play in comparison to the early '50s when every pot of colored paint was a hard-to-find item.

The novelty names of products say it all. Even George Nelson took time out from being design director at stylish Herman Miller (producers of Eames's furniture) to design his Marshmallow Sofa in 1956. This polka-dot-style sofa was made of standard bar-stool seats, covered in brightly colored vinyl on a metal frame. Surprisingly, only a few were put into production—it seems that even for the consumers hungry for novelty, this was a piece hard to live with every day. As Mark Burns so succinctly puts it in his book on '50s kitsch:

"The American living room is undeniably visually distracting, but it also has its own range of tactile and aural values. The faintly sweaty touch of vinyl is enlivened by the gentle hiss as you sink into the seat."

With the introduction of the television and record player to many homes, living rooms were filled with a glut of coffee tables. Organic shapes were popular, no doubt inspired by Neil Morris's cloud table of 1949. Some were designed to wrap around the corners of sofas and chairs to ensure that one's TV dinner was always within reach. The Parisian fad inspired artists' palettes and other curved designs were

based on boomerangs and less exotic kidneys (see pages 80–81 for details). These rounded forms wasted a lot of timber and were probably a reaction to the strict waste-not want-not philosophies of Utility furniture.

Triangular tables covered in contrasting laminates made a graphic harlequin detail when combined. All had legs of spindly metal or elegant tapered wood, often in threes. Another '50s design, thankfully now a thing of the past, is the phenomenon of the telephone table with its combined seat and telephone shelf, usually a superb synthetic combination of vinyl and Formica.

The final accessory for a modern retro living room must be a magazine rack, all the better if it can be painted in a gaudy abstract pattern or wrapped in zebra-skin plastic.

Today, search out funky colored tables and storage to add a quirky look to your living room. Alternatively add a plastic chair as a lighthearted counterpoint to serious upholstery or as a practical swivel chair in a home office. Robin Day's classic Polyprop chair has recently gone back into production, so for an original retro design snap up a pair in white, paprika, or sky blue. Another little polypropylene number is the award-winning Oh chair by Umbra Designs. Like the Polyprop, it's light, stackable, and sexy. It makes an excellent dining chair indoors or, as it is available in a choice of six rather subtle spacey colors, outside under the stars.

LEFT A turquoise molded plastic table, simply accessorized with an organic vase in Scandinavian '50s style and artificial roses.

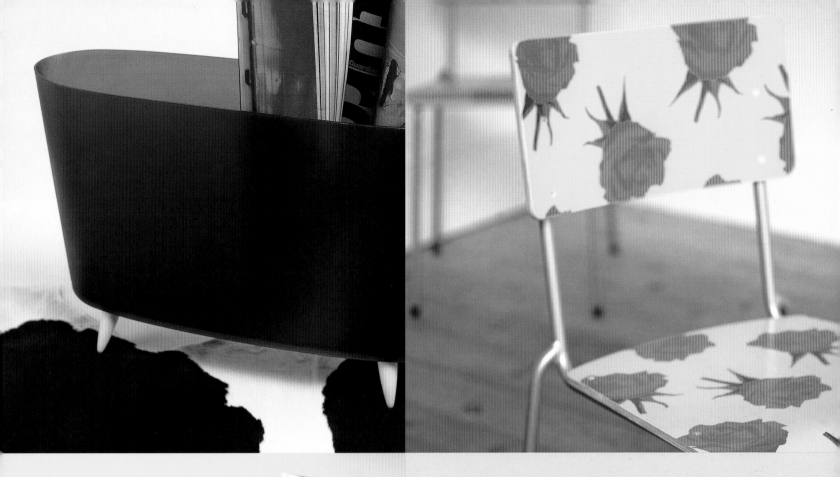

TOP LEFT On its own, the polypropylene magazine rack looks elegant. However, by combining it with a cow print rug, it looks more relaxed and borders on kitsch.

ABOVE Modern laminate chairs in startling colors and decorated with gaudy roses are no shrinking violets.

LEFT Nesting perspex tables in shocking pink demand to take center stage. The clean lines are emphasized by pulling the smaller tables forward.

FURNITURE 79

BOOMERANG COFFEE TABLE

In a throw-away world, the boomerang table should be a permanent addition for any retro interior.

1. Draw a gently curved three-sided shape on newspaper as a template. Make the template slightly smaller than the MDF. Cut out the template and place on the MDF. Secure it in position with masking tape and trace around the outline in pen.

2. Mark the position of the leg plates on the MDF, at least ¾in. from the edge. Secure the MDF to a workbench with a clamp, leaving the cutting edge free. Wearing the face mask and using a jigsaw, cut out the shape following the pen line. Drill leg plate holes. Rub down the cut edges with sandpaper.

3. Prime both sides of the table surface and table edge. When dry, paint with one or two coats of satinwood paint. Leave to dry thoroughly.

4. Screw the leg plates securely to the underside of the table and screw in the three legs.

YOU WILL NEED

Pencil, pen, and newspaper
Scissors
Sheet of ¾in.-thick MDF (medium density fibreboard) 18 × 24in.
Masking tape
Three metal table leg fittings and roundhead screws
Workbench and clamp
Face mask

Jigsaw
Wood drill
Sandpaper
Primer paint
Satinwood paint
Paintbrush
Three tapered legs
Screwdriver

TIPS

- Many hardware stores will cut the large sheets of MDF to smaller sizes to make them more portable.
- Leg plates are also available in an angled option. Instead of static legs, legs with castors are also available from stores such as IKEA.
- When priming and painting, put match sticks in the drilled holes to prevent them filling up with paint.
- Use the offcuts of MDF as swatches for painting with paint matchpots.
- Other common rounded '50s shapes include amoebae and artists' palettes. Alternatively, if you are not confident using a jigsaw, use a standard saw to cut a triangular shape.

WALLS & WINDOWS

"I like only those windows that face the sun."

Carl Larsson, Swedish artist

The opening up of interiors in the '50s combined with the trend for bigger windows meant that many homemakers had larger and lighter living spaces to decorate. Add to this the desire for modernity and contemporary furnishing schemes and a new style of decorating was created. In comparison to earlier fussy and formal schemes, the mood was for boldness and simplicity. It seems that we have now come full circle. After the flounces, frills, and general excesses of the '80s, we are returning to simpler solutions that are comfortable, practical, and individual. In essence, retro style revisited, revised, and recycled to make it suitable for contemporary homes.

LEFT Striking color schemes are best interpreted with utmost simplicity. Here a metal Venetian blind needs no further adornment.

DECORATING THE WALLS

During the '50s wallpapers and wall coverings regained their popularity. Using patterns similar to textile designs, the mood was bright. Popular patterns in Britain included natural motifs, abstract and scientific designs, graphic monochrome sun faces in the style of the Italian artist Piero Fornasetti, trellis designs and bold stripes. In the United States, wallpaper designs were even more lighthearted with large-scale fruit designs for the kitchen and cartoon characters often used in the family den or rumpus room. In Europe, the major market was Germany, where the emphasis was firmly on strong graphic designs, commonly on vinyl, which was wipe-clean. Major wallpaper companies such as Rasch had a very cosmopolitan outlook, commissioning many foreign designers, including Lucienne Day, to create patterns for them.

As a break away from traditional styles of decorating, the modern '50s home usually featured just one wall covered with wallpaper with the rest painted a contrasting color. If the paper design was particularly daring, it was often used on the alcove walls on either side of the fireplace, with a tiny, coordinating design for the chimney breast. This trend has been revived today as wallpapers replace the stippling and sponging paint crazes of the previous two decades.

Wallpapers are excellent for disguising less-than-perfect walls. For cool '50s appeal, look for papers with textural designs to complement large-scale fabric patterns. Natural images such as leaves, pebbles, or bamboo, or linear designs with a hand-drawn feel are all suitable for providing a calm background, which can be accessorized with classic retro pieces or contemporary designs with a '50s twist.

However, walls do not have to be covered with printed papers. Other recent trends ideal for retro interiors are textured and very tactile wall coverings, such as natural grass, hessian, raffia, or suede. The trick is not to use it on all four walls so that the room looks like a jungle tree house. And the ultimate touchy-feely wall covering must be paper-backed felt—ideal when hung on the wall behind a bed to create an oversize headboard.

For a more space-age or funky look, there are many papers on the market in sparkly metallic or shimmering holographic designs. Ideal when partnered with Bertoia or Saarinen wire and fiberglass furniture, they can be light and space-enhancing when used in small amounts.

WINDOW TREATMENTS

"Four walls and a roof overhead don't make for much of a home if there aren't any windows to let in a bit of the outside world."

Martha Stewart, American decorator

Before you decide how to tackle the decoration of your windows, first you need to assess your requirements. Start by removing any existing curtains or blinds and look critically at your naked windows. What shape and size are they? How are they spaced between walls and doors? Floor to ceiling? Are they inset or flush with the wall? Next, study the light and the view out of the window.

When do you most use the room—during the day, at night, continually? Is the room for relaxing or working? And finally, what can you see out of the window? Now you can start to look at various window treatments right for the room and your circumstances.

Generally three styles were favored for '50s windows—floor- or sill-length curtains in either a contemporary print or woven design; café curtains for kitchens and bathrooms in smaller prints or woven fabrics, especially gingham; and Venetian blinds, usually in metal or wood. Curtains were not often lined and were usually sewn with a simple gathered heading tape for hanging on tracks. Nylon net curtains, as beloved by suburbia, were not common until the end of the decade. Today, the choice is almost limitless in terms of fabrics, curtain heading styles, choices of poles or tracks, and blind types.

CHOOSING A STYLE

Careful treatment is needed for the large picture windows common to many postwar homes. First, it has to be a balance between privacy and coziness provided by curtains or blinds. You may not wish to cut out too much light, but also want some seclusion. Second, one must choose a fabric right for the style of the room, which does not end up looking like a set of stage curtains due to the volume of fabric, or like an explosion in a paint factory because of the dramatic design.

One solution might be to use sheer fabrics for privacy. Cotton and silk voiles are excellent for letting through some light while obscuring a poor view. If you don't want a wall of flat white fabric, choose voiles with a subtle white-on-white print, or dye natural voile or muslin for a gentle hint of color. Rather than sewing all the fabric widths into one curtain, an easier idea is to have individual curtains, possibly in alternating colors to give a wide striped effect. This also gives you the option of drawing or pulling curtains as required depending on the light. If you like the idea of individual curtains,

but want to stick to one color, sew horizontal tucks at intervals on each drape for added interest (remember to allow extra fabric on each length for this). To draw attention to a window, make it a focal point by decorating the organza or voile panel. In this situation the window panel should be the same width as the window, so that it hangs flat (see pages 88–89 for details).

Another option for semiprivacy for smaller paned windows is to attach sheets of opaque film to the lower panes, but leave the top ones uncovered. This a good idea for temporary apartments. A more permanent solution is to frost the glass.

For a large curtain, it may be tempting to select a small patterned fabric. However, when seen as a whole, the fabric design will appear overly fussy because of the large number of repeats. It is far better to choose a bolder design, as a large window will allow you to appreciate the scale of the pattern. In this scenario, the curtain fabric should be the first design choice as it can then act as the inspiration for the rest of the colors and textures in the room. If you try to find a suitable design after you have decorated, it will be far more difficult trying to tie all the elements together.

When there are small children about, a dramatic and practical solution in tall windowed rooms is to choose a plain fabric such as linen and then sew a wide contrasting border along the bottom. This border can be as much as a yard in depth and is ideal for disguising sticky marks. This is also a good way to use a small amount of a vintage fabric that you may have been lucky enough to acquire, which is not big enough on its own for a pair of curtains.

If you do wish to use old fabrics, always line the curtains or blinds to prevent any further fading. Fifties fabrics can be given a contemporary twist by choosing a modern heading style such as tab tops or large eyelets. Such headings give a simpler look as the curtain will generally hang flatter rather than puff out, as it might if sewn onto heading tape. If you are still anxious that the fabric design will be overpowering as curtains, opt for flat Roman blinds. Not only does this use less fabric, but also the design may look better as one is viewing it flat rather than as a rumpled curtain.

CHOOSING BLINDS

After their popularity in the '50s, blinds fell from favor in place of increasingly lavish curtains. Fortunately the trend has turned, as people rediscover their flexibility. Venetian blinds are now available in a range of colors in metal, plastic, or wood. They can be a great way to finish off a room without fuss or frills. Colored Venetian blinds can also be used as a neutral background, to coordinate or act as a dramatic contrast. Wooden blinds are ideal for retro rooms as they echo the slender wooden furniture designs, and give a warmer, cozier feel than metal or plastic versions.

LEFT Window treatments needn't be predictable. A series of sash windows are covered with simple roller blinds in contrasting colors with Perspex bars along the bottom edge.

RIGHT Disguise a boring view with a stunning voile panel. The circular designs on the fabric are echoed in the glass vase and ball-headed chrysanthemums.

Roman and roller blinds are a happy halfway stage—they appear softer than Venetian blinds because of the fabric, yet are still tailored, simple treatments for larger windows. For rooms with wide but shallow windows, a series of blinds will effectively break up the large expanse of glass. For added interest, do not have the blinds all unrolled to the same level—vary them according to the view and available daylight or to highlight any objects displayed next to the window.

If you are overlooked, think about reversing how your windows are covered. You can now buy blinds that are installed on the windowsill and work upside down. This allows valuable light in, but maintains a level of privacy. For window treatments with more punch, choose roller blinds, which have strips of acrylic inserted in the bottom hem. As the light shines through, you'll get flashes of jewel-bright color.

DOOR CURTAINS

The ultimate '50s kitsch "sun shade" must surely be the stringy plastic door curtain. If you are having difficulty tracking down an original, choose a modern one made with plastic beads, or make your own hip version using plastic drinking straws strung end to end on fishing nylon. If this sounds too "plastic fantastic," another more stylish idea is to attach long lengths of ribbon in various widths, colors, and designs to a piece of dowel rod and fit it above your door. The ribbon treatment is also good for decorating windows in the summer. Simply tie the ribbons to the curtain pole, open the window, and watch them flutter gently in the breeze—definitely prettier and less irritating than the constant tinkle of wind chimes.

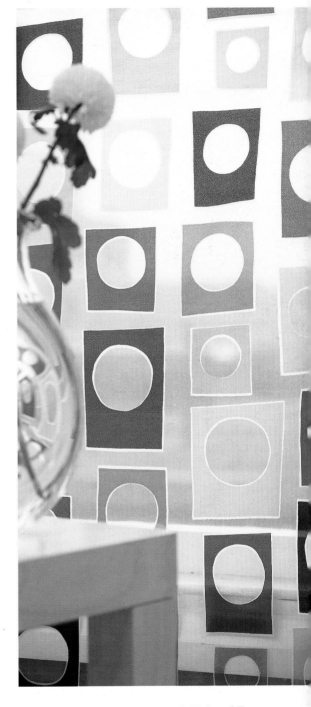

ROSE VOILE WINDOW PANEL

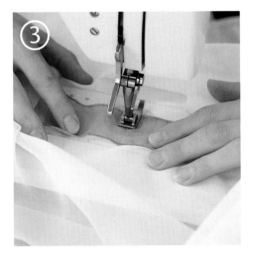

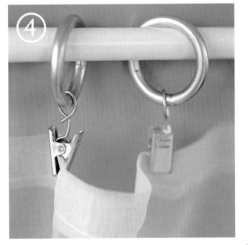

Turn an urban view into a rural paradise with this organza panel. Ideal for armchair gardeners everywhere.

1. Iron and sew a narrow hem down the side lengths of the organza. Iron and sew a top and bottom hem, folding over a total of 2 in. at each end. Iron the organza. Trim the rose stems to about 10 in. and position the flowers evenly over the panel.

2. Cut the ribbon into 5in. lengths. Place a length of ribbon under each rose stem just below the flower. Pin the ribbon to the organza.

3. Remove the roses and machine-stitch vertically down the centre of each ribbon length using matching thread.

4. Attach the roses to the panel by twisting the ribbon around each rose stem. Clip the curtain clips evenly along the top hem of the panel, and slide onto the curtain pole. Bend each rose stem slightly so the bloom faces forward.

YOU WILL NEED

2¼yd. of organza 48in. wide
Iron
Sewing machine
Thread to match the organza and ribbon
Fifteen artificial roses in assorted colors
Ruler
Sharp scissors

1⅞yd. of wire-edged organza ribbon 1½in. wide
Pins
Twelve curtain clips

TIPS

- Any artificial flowers (or greenery) are suitable as long as the blooms are not too large and heavy.
- Change the flowers in winter and summer to suit the seasons.
- The finished length of this panel is 2yd, but it can be adapted to fit any window. Simply measure the finished drop and add 4in. to this measurement for top and bottom hems.
- Instead of using curtain clips, make the top hem deeper and thread the pole directly through the curtain panel.

SOFT FURNISHINGS

"It was such a lovely day – I thought it was a pity to get up."

Somerset Maugham, English writer

As we spend a large proportion of our time in bed, the bedroom really should be a refuge and comfort zone. There is nothing more decadent than sleeping in or breakfast in bed, and at the other end of the day, the bliss of curling up in crisp cotton sheets fresh from a breezy clothesline is sublime. Today, the choice of bed linens is far better than in the '50s, when the height of modernity was a nylon sheet. Today, a combination of duvets, sheets, pillows, and cushions of all shapes and sizes, topped with quilts and throws, make a bed plump and welcoming.

THE LINEN CUPBOARD LOOK

The first stage to creating a retro bedroom is to consider the essentials—the bed and the storage. Start with an iron bedstead (still to be found in junk shops and architectural salvage yards relatively inexpensively). Repaint or polish and buy a new mattress to fit. Alternatively, metal bed frames in brushed aluminium as well as the more common iron can be found in many high-street stores. Instead of the '50s penchant for old blankets to soften a hard mattress, choose a mattress pad or wool fleece mattress cover. Finally, top with flat sheets (see pages 96–97 for details), neatly folded duvets, and plump pillows. Just like the layering principle for clothes, top up the bed linen in winter with cotton or chenille throws or a cosy patchwork quilt. However, make sure the top layer isn't too heavy, otherwise the air will be squashed from the duvet and it will not be as efficient. On extra cold nights, add a hot-water bottle—much more toasty and less drying than the bland heat of central heating.

For a restful, uncluttered bedroom, keep other furniture to a minimum. For storage, hunt out vintage kitchen or pantry cabinets. These often

ABOVE Mix small and large woven checks with floral bed linen to create a bedroom with an authentic retro feel.

LEFT Pillows with an Oxford border look much more luxurious than housewife styles, but require only a little extra fabric. Make your own using gingham and white sheeting (see pages 96–97 for details on how to create these borders).

have glass doors or slatted wooden shelves and make ideal linen cupboards. Paint with a fresh coat of satinwood paint and add new handles if necessary. Clean bed linen and spare quilts or pillows are kept smelling sweet by being spritzed with lavender water as they are ironed or by hanging herbal sachets in the closet. For dirty laundry, sew drawstring bags (like oversized school gym bags) from remnants of jolly fabric, or use a wicker chest such as those still manufactured by Lusty's Lloyd Loom.

To store smaller items, cover archive boxes from office stationers with wallpaper in retro patterns and trim with satin ribbon. Even if the contents are more prosaic, such as bank statements instead of love letters, at least the box is romantic.

SCANDINAVIAN STYLE

If, however, all these floral patterns are likely to bring on an attack of hay fever, opt for a calm and restful Scandinavian-inspired bedroom instead. Keep colors light and natural and aim for an interesting contrast of textures—rough and smooth, matt and shiny. If using wallpaper, choose a small geometric design or a leaf motif. The colors should be very subtle and for a more contemporary look, keep the paper to one wall only with the remaining walls in a matching paint color. Choose a laminate floor, coir floor covering, or bouclé wool carpet, with a ribbed chenille runner for soft landings on either side of the bed.

The bed itself should be as simple as possible—opt for either a box frame or modern wood base, maybe with a headboard made of interwoven tapes. Choose soft unbleached bed linen, pillows in a multitude of shapes, and a plump feather duvet. Top with a colored throw in a rich cream or rice-field green, a bedspread with a subtle pin-tucking, or a single color quilt.

Keep any window treatments minimal, such as wooden Venetian blinds, or a bamboo roller blind if working on a tight budget. A vintage sideboard with its sleek boxy lines would provide excellent storage space for jumpers and T-shirts with space for shoes underneath. Alternatively, hunt out Utility desks as alternative dressing tables. Simple ply tables shaped like an upturned U make ideal side tables for the bed.

Accessories should be pared down as the finished look needs to be spare and sophisticated. Choose wooden lamp bases in solid drum or sinuous hourglass shapes with raffia, basketweave, or hessian shades. A metal wall clock with a face in a classic '50s typeface

and a collection of studio pottery in grays, browns, and creams arranged in small groups help to create a calm yet comfortable bedroom.

If this scheme feels too safe, hunt out one stunning piece of furniture such as a chrome Bertoia chair or a classic Danish design. However, remember such a gem should be positioned near a sunny window for maximum effect and usage and not used as a general dumping ground for discarded clothes.

QUILTS AND BLANKETS

Although patchwork and quilting were not as popular in the '50s as they are today, patchwork quilts look completely at home in a retro bedroom. If you are lucky, you may have received an old well-loved family quilt. If not, it's easy to sew your own heirloom using cotton fabric and cotton or polyester batting. If you are a beginner to this craft, stick to simple shapes like squares or stripes, which can be pieced together by machine, and simply hand quilted in a straightforward grid design.

Before duvets were introduced in the '70s, beds were a layered affair with blankets, bedspreads, or eiderdowns. Today the layers are there more for decoration than for warmth. Bedspreads have reduced in size to become throws and '50s candlewick has largely been replaced by cotton chenille, which makes a decadent bed throw. For an efficient yet stylish alternative to a blanket, buy a length of fleece material and blanket-stitch the edges in a contrasting color. Fleece is much lighter in weight than a blanket, but is very efficient at thermal insulation, plus it washes and dries like a dream—polyester has never looked so stylish!

FAR LEFT A vintage kitchen cabinet finds a new lease on life as a linen cupboard. This model still has its original etched glass and melamine handles.

LEFT Colorful patchwork quilts sewn from a collection of '50s gingham napkins and retro-inspired floral fabrics. Stored quilts should be re-folded at intervals to prevent creases forming.

ABOVE Cozy wool blankets in cheery checks are ideal for an extra layer of warmth, and they lift the spirits even on the coldest mornings.

CUSHIONS AND OTHER COMFORTS

Soft furnishings are a quick and easy way to give a living room a comfortable, lived-in appeal. Throws and slipcovers are an ideal way of disguising hand-me-down sofas, which may be structurally sound but don't fit into your present color scheme. Even if your sofa is new, throws can also give a seasonal look to the room. Choose thick chenille and velvet for a cozy winter feel, and lighter cotton or raw silk for summer.

For a modern take on antimacassars, which give a more tailored effect than a throw, drape a narrow length of fabric or folded blanket down the back of the chair, across the seat and toward the floor. This can look particularly effective if you play with colors and textures. For a streamlined look, the fabric should not be the full width of the chair, leave about three inches on either side. Possible combinations on solid-color sofas include black and white ticking, a vibrant flower design, a length of fake fur, or a vintage fabric length in a bold design.

A pile of cushions also encourages relaxation. While they can be pricey to buy as they require so little fabric (about eighteen inches per cushion), they are inexpensive and simple to make—look at housewife pillowcases, for the easiest construction technique. Don't just restrict yourself to home-furnishing fabrics—there are often some really unusual materials to be found in dress-fabric stores. Some ideas include:

- Recycle vintage buttons (every family has a button tin somewhere full of odd orphan buttons). Use as decorative fastenings on plain linen or brushed cotton cushion covers. Or, if they deserve center stage,

make a feature of them. Using a running stitch, hand-sew a grid on the cushion front in thicker thread. Sew a button in the centre of each square. The size of the squares depends on the size of buttons chosen. For buttons about three-eighths of an inch, make the squares about two inches large. If you come across retro buttons or other haberdashery items still on their original cards, it is best to leave them as they are.

- Charmeuse satins, velvet, crinkly polyesters, and organza are ideal for cushions and bolsters in Hollywood-style boudoirs, where luxury is the key feature.

- Hand-dye calico for a good selection of colors to fit in with your '50s color scheme. Hand-dyeing gives a glorious richness to the color, not seen on yarn-dyed cloth. If you use the same dye bath for several pieces of fabric, each will be a little paler than the last, giving a subtle, toning look.

- Hunt out narrow-width materials such as roller toweling fabric, which is great for utility-style cushions in a kitchen. Deck chair canvas is tough and ideal for cushions for the garden. Choose striped designs for an authentic "end of the pier" look.

- Appliqué '50s iconic images such as atomic motifs or anything space age onto plain cottons (see pages 50–51).

- Polyester fleece is one of the wonder fabrics of the last decade. It's a dream to sew, so make oversized, super-soft cushions, perfect for snuggling into or for throwing onto the floor as extra seating.

- Mock suede is great for modern-look

cushions in a family home as the fabric is usually washable.

- Pinstripe suitings and tweedy wools are ideal for more tailored interiors such as those inspired by '50s coffee culture (see page 104). The emphasis should be on subtle woven fabric designs and crisp, clean cushion styles.

- If you are an expert with knitting needles, rustle up a couple of cushion covers instead of a twinset. Knitwear is big news again on the catwalks and the look is filtering through into home design. Bar-code stripes in candy colors are a good way to use up odd balls of wool. For a more subtle effect, use two colors only to create a bold fifty-fifty stripe. For more ideas, see Chapter 10 if you would rather salvage than knit your own creations.

- Crocheted throws made of bull's eye squares may bring back memories of textile projects in junior high school, however they are extremely chic right now and cannot be bettered as retro accessories. For a more sophisticated look (rather than the usual student or granny effect), plan the color scheme in advance, just as you would a patchwork quilt. Monochromes, a selection of natural tones or contrasting colors such as a range of blues with just a small amount of burnt orange or terra-cotta would all look stunning made in cotton yarns.

RIGHT Fifties curtain fabric converted into scatter cushions jazz up an otherwise unremarkable sofa. The fronts and backs of cushions need not be made from the same fabric if you are eeking out a small remnant.

GINGHAM-TRIMMED BED LINEN

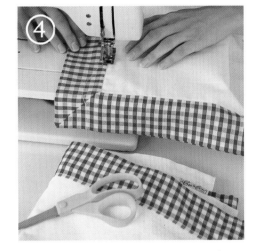

A bold border in cheerful red gingham spices up plain white bed linen.

1. Pin and sew the eight short lengths of gingham onto the short sides of the two smaller pieces of sheeting, with an even amount of excess gingham at each end. Press the seams towards the gingham. Cut the larger pillowcase shapes into two, 10in. from the end. Fold over the cut edges twice, iron and sew a hem, making sure that the wrong side of the hem is on the same side of fabrics as the raw seams of the gingham.

2. With the hemmed sides of the pillowcase on top, place the back and front pieces of the pillowcase together, right sides facing. Match and pin at the corners. This will give you the correct amount of overlap for the pillowcase flap. Pin the overlapping flaps together. Remove the corner pins, separate the front and the back, and sew the flap part together along the overlapping white sheeting.

3. Sew the eight long gingham lengths to the long sides of the pillowcases, stopping the stitching at the edge of the sheeting, with an even amount of excess gingham at each end. Press seams toward the gingham. Sew the four mitred corners on each pillowcase by folding each corner of the sheet in at a 45-degree angle. Stitch the gingham from the corner of the pillowcase to the edge. Iron. Trim off surplus fabric underneath.

4. Pin the two sides of the pillowcase together, right sides facing. Sew around the edge of the gingham. Turn to the right side and iron. Pin and top-stitch again around the edge of the sheeting at the seam with the gingham to give the flange. The sheet is trimmed by ironing a centre fold and a $\frac{1}{2}$in hem along the edges of the gingham. Pin along the top edge of the sheet, folding in a narrow hem at each end. Top-stitch and iron.

YOU WILL NEED

(for two pillowcases and one double sheet)

$^3/_4$yd of gingham 45in wide, cut as follows: eight strips 3 × 27in. and eight strips 3 x 35in. Cut the remaining gingham into two strips 6 $^1/_4$ × 45in. and sew together as one long strip.

1yd of white sheeting 109in wide, cut into two pieces 20 x 28in. and two pieces 20 × 33in.

Tape measure
Scissors
Pins
Iron
Sewing machine
White thread
White double flat sheet

KITCHENS & TABLEWARE

"One cannot think well,

love well,

sleep well,

if one has not dined well."

Virginia Woolf, English writer

During the '50s there was a great change in attitude toward living spaces in the home, particularly kitchens. During the war, many women had worked outside the home. Although the majority became full-time housewives again after 1945, their attitude to homemaking had changed. They wanted to reduce the drudgery of household chores as much as possible to leave time for the more enjoyable aspects of homemaking. As a result, kitchens became more ergonomic, easier to look after, and generally colorful and comfortable rooms in which to work. Domestic appliances, large and small, flooded the market and were snapped up. As living spaces, kitchens opened up—new housing developments often had large open-plan kitchen-dining-living rooms replacing the formal front room, small kitchen, and scullery. Because of new developments in plastics and laminates, kitchens became bright and breezy rooms, filled with a host of gadgetry, jolly china, colorful packaging, and wipe-clean surfaces.

Today kitchens remain the hub of many houses. For a retro-style kitchen, it is not necessary to forsake the computerized washer-dryer in place of an ancient twin tub. However, pure functionalism should be joined by a sense of individuality for a kitchen filled with wit, comfort, and personality.

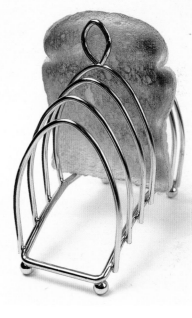

ABOVE No kitchen table is complete without a toast rack. It also prevents the toast from getting soggy as it cools.

OPPOSITE A conventional kitchen has potential to become a '50s kitchenette with the addition of a vinyl floor, diner furniture, a classic drop-leaf pantry cupboard, and a large dose of melamine.

LEFT It's always time for tea and cake with this automobile-inspired kitchen clock.

Diner chic

"If Hollywood is to be believed, diner fare's the food that built America."

Melina Keays, food writer

Coffee bars, milk bars, and diners are all synonymous with the '50s. Distinctly American in the '50s, diners were pit stops for both truck drivers and mom-and-pop family outings. Often standing alone, the aluminium-and-chrome belles were an enthusiastic celebration of fresh fast food, countless cups of coffee, and a warm welcome any time of day or night. Today diners are found worldwide, an individual alternative to soulless fast-food chains. Their functional, bold design has permeated through to the home.

The elements of diner chic are easy to master—functional, mass-produced

LEFT Diner furniture is as American as apple pie, and is usually a celebration of wipe-clean laminates and chromed metal. These diner mugs are typical of those used daily by thousands of Americans

THIS PAGE Typical diner accessories, such as these tomato ketchup and honey pots, ensure that everything to season or sweeten the meal is within easy reach.

utility items, bold colors with easy-to-clean vinyl, Formica and stainless steel being the essential materials. Start with the floor, in vinyl, rubber, or ceramic tiles in bright checks. Next, add a traditional diner table and chairs. These beauties with their chrome edging and overstuffed seats hark back to days when the automobile was king with tail fins and plenty of chromium plating. In a small apartment, a bar and stools offer an alternative, authentic diner feel.

Appliances in the retro-style kitchen should be functional and made of stainless steel. Classic blenders and toasters efficiently earn their keep and look good at the same time. Inexpensive spun aluminium pendants make excellent "diner" lamps—hang several in a straight line over a dining table or work counter. Choose extra large wall clocks with plastic or metal rims and clear faces as time as paramount in a busy diner.

Finally, add the accessories—this is definitely the fun part. Diner-style china and glassware can be bought inexpensively from junk shops, catering suppliers, or lifestyle stores depending on your taste and budget. China should be plain white, institutional green, or white with simple chef checks, rim lines, or diner logos as decoration. Always choose mugs or jumbo cups and saucers (diner style is never delicate). Dinner plates and soup or dessert bowls must be oversized to allow for healthy pit-stop portions. Any authentic diner will also have choice

phrases dotted around the place such as "Clean as a whistle," "Johnny Rockets hits the spot," "Good and wholesome always," "No dancin' in the aisles," or "Take outs are fine, but please leave the tables and chair." Create your own unique diner china by painting your favourite phrases onto plain china plates or mugs (see pages 112–113 for instructions)

In diners, cutlery is invariably a simple, stainless-steel design that is dishwasher-safe. For domestic kitchens, colored or checkered handles can echo the china designs. And finally, remember that the soda glassware is often faceted, usually branded with unintelligible names such as "Harley cooler" or "Lexington hiball" and is always extra large to allow space for plenty of ice cubes.

Eating in a diner environment should be casual and unfussy. Keep table decoration to a minimum—a single bloom set in a glass milk bottle, condiments all stacked together on a tray, and napkins made either from solid-color waffle-weave fabric or checked tea towels are all that's needed to compliment the surroundings.

The pièce de résistance would of course be a tabletop jukebox, such as the Seeburg Wall-o-matic, belting out Elvis Presley or Doris Day hits. Songs like these are decidedly more in keeping with authentic diner style than the local radio station. However, if it has to be the latter, at least make sure that you choose a retro-style radio to enable you to jitterbug around the toaster.

Fishs Eddy, purveyors of sturdy-ware

Fishs Eddy is a store like no other in New York. It is named after the proprietors' favorite trout fishing town on Route 17 in upstate New York. For lovers of dinerware it is a pit stop in diner heaven. Originally specializing in country-style antiques, the current retro range came about by accident. Out on a buying trip on the back roads of the midwest in their blue Ford pickup, the owners came across a fire-damaged warehouse. Stacked to what remained of the rafters were piles of unused commercial china, covered in soot but otherwise undamaged. Hauled back to New York and cleaned up, the china went on sale and as word spread the stock rapidly depleted.

All the mid-century china was American, made originally for a variety of customers—roadside diners, country clubs, and university dining halls. Some was elegant but the majority was sturdy, everyday stoneware with cheerful logos such as "Try our coffee—it's delicious!" or "Cup of Joe to go." Another classic design is the blue plate special, which diners used for the special or dish of the day. Much was made by Homer Laughlin China in Ohio, a pottery company specializing in vitrified china for the restaurant and hotel market.

Since that first haul, Fishs Eddy has continued to uncover gems from the past. Because of the demand for functional retroware, the store has now designed its own range of dinerware, including the 212 range, which has a skyscraper skyline of New York around the rim and the Dining Car range featuring an aerodynamic railroad car.

No diner would be complete without a range of everyday, hard-wearing glassware stacked on glass and chrome shelves against mirrored walls. Fishs Eddy is no exception. Its shelves groan under the rows and rows of soda glasses, sundae dishes, sugar pourers, coolers, rocks, hiballs, and juice glasses with jaunty logos such as "Drink Cheer Up."

The best thing about the Fishs Eddy collection is that it's very definitely non-precious, practical, affordable and fun. As the owners state: "We believe an entire century of making dishes the same way is proof positive; there is simply no replacement for classic shapes and beautiful design."

TOP LEFT The 'Drink Cheer Up' glass is typical of '50s diner glasses with simple motifs silk-screened onto the glass. In recent years manufacturers have rediscovered the simple graphic impact of printed glassware.

TOP RIGHT Chrome and glass sugar pourers and syrup drizzlers—typical accessories.

BOTTOM LEFT Stackable glassware is synonymous with a diner environment. Available in a variety of sizes and so tough it almost bounces, it's ideal for the family home.

BOTTOM RIGHT Essential on any diner counter, the glass and chrome straw dispenser comes in handy for shakes, malts, and ice-cream floats.

RIGHT Upbeat logos on diner mugs keep customers "on the ball" and "on the move." The 212 line from Fishs Eddy features Manhattan skycrapers.

Coffee bar culture

To cater to the increasing number of young people in the '50s wanting somewhere to meet, there was a huge growth in the number of Italian coffee bars in Britain. Unlike the wholesome environment of milk bars, coffee bars were thought (by the older generation) to be highly dubious centers for youth culture. As such, they were extremely popular!

Coffee bars were seen as sophisticated and "continental" with huge Gaggia machines pumping out espressos and cappuccinos or "froffy coffee" as it was called. It was a marked contrast to the typical prewar "greasy spoon caff." The coffee bar clientele was a mixture of beatniks and young men and women relaxing after work.

At the turn of a new century, coffee bars are once again popular, except today's café society is more likely to be surfing on the Internet than discussing Sartre or Sagan. However, today coffee culture is not just about socializing but is also influencing home design, with deep browns and rich creams at the forefront of interior collections. Just as in coffee bars, when all the senses are stimulated—the sound of the steaming milk, the animated discussions, the smell of the cinnamon and the final decadent spooning and tasting of a cappuccino—interior design is as much about touching, feeling, tasting, and smelling as visual satisfaction.

The café society look is ideally suited to living and dining areas. Include elements of Scandinavian contemporary for a distinctly European look of understated luxury—suede, leather, and jumbo cord upholstery, mixed with wool cushions and raw silk throws. Wenge wood competes with blond birch or classic teak for storage and table designs. Classic products from the '50s such as Noguchi lamps, Wegner chairs and Day's sumptuous leather upholstery are casually combined with contemporary designs. Assembling this look should not be instant, but a slow, rich blend of elements. And finally, whatever you economize on, buy the best coffee you can.

LEFT The bold graphics on these mugs inject a witty note to an early cup of tea.

Milk bars

If coffee bars catered to the young sophisticates, milk bars were where teenagers gathered to eat-in, hang out, and catch up with gossip. Milk bars and ice-cream parlors may seem terribly dated with their images of wholesome teenagers in full skirts, knitted twinsets, chinos, and checked shirts. However the soda fountain color palette is a perennial '50s favorite enjoying a particular revival right now.

When combined with plenty of soft white, watermelon, coral pink, banana yellow and pistachio green, the look is fun, feminine, and flirty without being fluffy. The trick is to use the milk-bar pastels in slightly chalky tones, rather than sugary shades. Capture the look with limed wood floors and walls painted with chalky water-based paints. Try not to obscure windows—this look is all about light. Window

treatments should be kept simple—roman blinds in organza or plain linen are ideal.

To give the accessories a neutral background, choose or paint kitchen units in soft white. Colored metal or marble-topped bistro tables continue the café feel, and are ideal for small kitchens. Folding garden chairs are also great space savers, and can be made more comfortable with simple tied cushions made in an assortment of colors. Buy a little extra fabric and use the surplus for napkins or table runners as an alternative to full tablecloths.

The china used for milk-bar kitchens can be a hodgepodge of plain white porcelain and a smattering of rainbow-colored earthenware reminiscent of the famous Fiestaware china popular throughout the '50s (see page 106). For an individual look, combine the classic Fiesta colors of persimmon, rose, chartreuse, turquoise, and periwinkle blue. Keep the ceramics plain as including floral patterns would tip the balance into cloying sweetness. Remember the look should be bohemian modern romantic rather than high school prom queen. If you can find vintage cutlery with plastic handles, this is ideal. Alternatively, choose simple modern designs with clear or colored acrylic handles.

Other essential items for the milk bar look include a blender for whipping up shakes, fruit flips, and the like, plus a ready supply of glassware. Glasses should be plain and simple. Mix colored stemware in turquoise, gray, or amethyst with clear and frosted heavy-based tumblers. Such designs, typical of Scandinavian glass of the '50s, are still manufactured by Orrefors and Boda Nova in Sweden and Ittala in Finland among others. Alternatively, jazz up unremarkable glassware with subtle frosting (see pages 136–137 for

details on frosting). The final touch should be an oversized, gently rounded pastel fridge with chrome detailing. Such beauties are available new with authentic retro styling; alternatively, reconditioned vintage models that are CFC-free for a second burst of life in a new millennium are available from specialty mail-order companies.

LEFT AND RIGHT Just the thing to start or end a busy day. Keep a snazzy blender on the worktop so you can whip up a strawberry shake in seconds.

BELOW The Dualit is the Rolls Royce of the toaster world. Available in shiny chrome or '50s pastels, it's a must-have item for every retro-style kitchen.

Retro style served up on a plate

Fifties tableware designs are a microcosm of '50s passions. Worldwide, the style of tableware was shifting away from the formal fine china services of previous decades to more colorful and casual designs. In Britain, the Council of Industrial Design (advisors to the government's wartime rationing program) hoped that after a decade of plain white china, consumers' taste would be converted to the modernist designs Utility promoted, rather than the gaudy legacy of art deco. However, this was in vain and younger people were hungry for the colorful, quirkily decorated earthenware when it became available. In the meantime, resourceful homemakers covered plain china with waterproof transfers, which were sold at events like the Ideal Home Exhibition.

There were five main styles for printed and decorated china:

- Abstract designs, strongly influenced by Cubist artists such as Picasso and Braque.

- Stylized and dissected versions of natural images such as fruits and leaves.

- The influence of foreign travel, as discussed in Chapter 3.

- The studio pottery movement, especially strong in Scandinavia.

- The influence of modern science as demonstrated by the crystallography designs of the Festival Pattern Group.

In the United States, one of the best known retro designs is Fiesta made by the Homer Laughlin company. In fact this range isn't really '50s at all—it was launched in 1936 and if you look closely at its ridged and rounded silhouette, you can see its art deco origins. However, demand for this chunky, rainbow-bright china peaked during the '50s. Discontinued in 1973, Homer Laughlin reissued it on its fiftieth anniversary, the designs unaltered, but with new glaze colors. Currently there are nine colors in production, including such '50s classics as persimmon (an orangey-red), chartreuse (soft lime), turquoise, and butter yellow. Today, it is one of the most collected china designs in the world, and its cheery nature cannot help but lift the spirits on a dull day.

Fifties china is one of the easiest retro items to find. As china is easily broken and sets become fragmented, the orphans regularly turn up in charity shops and junk stores, usually for pennies unless they are one of the classic patterns, such as Homemaker or by well-known designers like Susie Cooper and Terence Conran. Look out for the following key pottery names that were prolific in the '50s: Midwinter, Poole, Ridgway, Swinnertons, and Arthur Meakin.

Unless you are a dedicated and patient collector, do not try to assemble a complete service in one design, but mix and match different patterns, maybe concentrating on a color, or a style such as checks, poodles, or leaves. Mix '50s china in with contemporary ranges and if at all possible, display your collection on open shelves or in glass-fronted cupboards so that the dolly mixture effect can be enjoyed.

TOP LEFT Part of a mix-and-match rainbow tea-set purchased in 1954.

TOP RIGHT Melamine was as popular as earthenware for everyday tableware, and often as expensive.

BOTTOM Two contemporary Fiesta ware pitchers showing their classic curves and ridged design.

RIGHT Typical of '50s ceramic patterns, this leaf design is spare and reduced to its essential elements.

MARIE PEPPERCORN (1971–)

"My ceramics provide a canvas for my designs. As wall-hung pieces, they're like an extension of my etchings—although they can be eaten off too."

Just as in the '50s, when designers frequently used surface pattern designs across different media, Marie Peppercorn continues this design practice today. Coming from a fine-art background, she studied printmaking at the University of Central Lancashire. This course enabled her to experiment with pattern-making on various media, and she found that working with three-dimensional surfaces suited her designs best. A post-graduate ceramics course at Staffordshire University, in the heart of "British pottery country," allowed her to explore this further.

RETRO REFINEMENT

Her ceramics are a fine example of '50s retro with a '90s twist. Just as in the '50s when experimental companies such as David Whitehead used fine artists like Henry Moore and John Piper to design for textiles and ceramics, Peppercorn's designs translate well on to different media. The original idea came from the flat decorative plates that '50s homemakers put on their walls. She has designed countless patterns for china, all working with a restrained color palette of white, lilac, light purple, lemon, aqua, and black. The ceramics are covered with graphic geometric patterns often on a patchwork background. They are also liberally scattered with spindly classic designs from the '50s—Race's Antelope chair, Jacobsen's three-legged Ant chair, plus the more fluid S chair from Verner Panton.

As many ceramic designers also discovered fifty years ago, Peppercorn uses a coupe (rimless) shape. This provides a simple base for her designs, which suit the casual, yet sophisticated, look. Her cups and saucers (with different patterns on each part) use a classic can shape, which allows the pattern to take center stage. Her ceramics collection is designed to mix and not quite match, a concept consumers today are embracing with ease. However, for young homemakers in the '50s this idea of one set of brightly patterned earthenware china for everyday dining and entertaining was seen as quite "modern," as it was a world away from the "best china" syndrome of their parents' generation.

Peppercorn's quirky designs bring to mind the classic Homemaker range designed by Enid Seeney for Woolworths in the mid-1950s. However, while Homemaker instantly says '50s, Peppercorn's work is undeniably from the late '90s. Perhaps it is the more refined color palette, maybe it is because there is such a comprehensive collection—the consumer needs to have the confidence to pick and chose their collection. Peppercorn's tableware is complemented by sinuous, feminine vases with hourglass figures and a textile collection, handprinted on linen.

Another distinct difference from ceramics in the '50s is the difficulty young designers have today getting their work produced on a commercial basis. When manufacturing constraints were lifted from the ceramics industry in the early '50s, potteries were falling over themselves to introduce contemporary designs. However, in today's global market it is increasingly difficult for manufacturers to invest money in such a comprehensive and labor-intensive collection. As a result, Peppercorn's work, although gathering recognition across Europe and the United States, is produced on a small scale, and therefore remains more expensive than mass-market ranges. However, Peppercorn remains upbeat about this—the small scale means that her designs are produced as limited editions.

As she explains: "In the '80s and early '90s people wanted a very slick finish, but now they are after more original work. The late '90s consumer wants utility with style."

In a nutshell, Peppercorn has summed up the mood of interior design now. Homes can take inspiration from a variety of sources and should be an eclectic expression of a person's individuality.

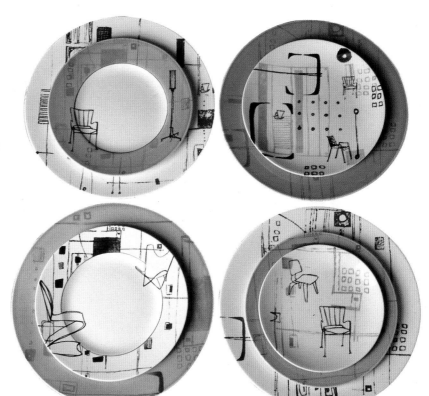

LEFT, ABOVE AND BELOW Marie Peppercorn's contemporary retro ceramics aptly summarize the mood and fashions of the '50s. Furniture icons sit cheek by jowl with scratched and spacey patterns, all captured in a '50s color palette.

The appliance of science

"Electricity is truly a wonderful and well-organised thing."

1949 British advertisement extolling the virtues of "modern energy" and electric kettles, even if they were only obtainable after a considerable wait.

BELOW A sleek stainless steel kettle is prevented from taking itself too seriously with a stay-cool plastic handle and knob to coordinate with the gingham oilcloth.

ABOVE RIGHT This citrus juicer is as functional as it is stylish and proves that not every gadget has to be electrical.

By the early '50s, the United States was way ahead of Europe in terms of gadgetry for the kitchen. British housewives could only admire the sophistication of American "dream" kitchens with their state-of-the-art refrigerator, washing machines, and small appliances. In Britain, although 48 percent of homes had electricity, they had little to plug in. Even after the war had ended, British manufacturers were forced to concentrate on a massive export drive in an effort to clear the war debt. The phrase "jam tomorrow" was coined by advertisers to tell of good times around the corner and to apologize to consumers for the long delay.

So when products finally became available in the early '50s, there was a massive consumer boom and spending spree (often on hire purchase terms) in Britain, as homemakers here raced to catch up.

Suddenly, kitchens became a shrine to all things electrical—food mixers, twin-tub washers, electric kettles, espresso coffee makers, heated food trays, and hostess trolleys. The ultimate of all appliances, however, must surely be the Goblin Cheerywake teasmade for the suburban bedroom. What decadence!

Consumers continued to spend throughout the '50s; in fact American manufacturers encouraged planned obsolescence so that there was a continual trading up to the latest restyled or new-and-improved wonder product. The kitchen was a rainbow of modernity as many products, such as the Servis washer, came in a selection of "fabulous gaytone colors!—guardsman red, almond green, horizon blue, and lemon-peel yellow teamed with white or cream." No wonder '50s housewives always looked so deliriously happy in the advertisements with such a push-button, multicolored world at their perfectly manicured fingertips.

However, after this explosion of innovative gadgetry, the past twenty-five years has seen the design of kitchen appliances plunge to new depths, with a profusion of drab rustic designs appearing on mass-market ranges in an attempt, for some reason, to disguise functional kettles as wheat sheaves, or to coordinate an entire kitchen as a bouquet of summer flowers. Fortunately for retro devotees, kitchen accessory manufacturers are finally concentrating once again purely on color and shape, steering clear of such dubious motifs.

Nowadays, it has never been easier to accessorize your kitchen with retro-style appliances. In recent years, everything electrical seems to have had a '50s makeover in an attempt to make high-tech look homely but not trite. Kettles, irons, and toasters are popping up in pastel shades, whether they are plastic or metal.

However, if pastels aren't your thing, other manufacturers are producing appliances in translucent plastics and jelly-bean bright colors. You want a tomato-red, orange, or

RIGHT Like other brands of this era, the Dualit toaster with its rounded curves and maraschino cherry handle has become a classic.

FAR RIGHT Modern appliances hark back to the '50s in their shapes and colors.

apple-green kettle? It's out there somewhere. The good news is that these innovations are not at an exclusive designer level but available in the high street. Of course a few items such

as the Waring blender and KitchenAid food mixer have not needed an overhaul. Their original styling remains intact and bears a testament to their classic design as they continue to appeal to serious and stylish cooks.

Apart from these electrical appliances, other kitchen accessories can be just as quirky as practical in the retro kitchen, such as juicers resembling plastic cacti or shiny chrome insects, neon-hued plastic chopping boards, and kitchen scales formally called Dolly and in pastel twinset colors.

As kitchens continue to be multi-functional rooms at the hub of the household, why not include an I-mac computer in a matching shade? It may be idiosyncratic but is certainly less offensive than a teasmade and can always be put to good use ordering your groceries online. Technology not just tamed but also house-trained.

PAINTED PLATES

Create your own "diner china" by painting designs onto plain white plates.

1. Doodle on paper to work out designs. Keep images simple and remember that if you paint over the whole surface of the plate, most will be hidden by the food! Most paint manufacturers recommend that you do not cut directly on a painted surface as this can mark the design. If using several sizes of plates, use complementary but different designs.

2 Odd plates can be picked up cheaply at garage sales and charity shops, so use these first to experiment with designs or to practice your technique. Wash and dry crockery thoroughly before painting.

3. Using the tube of outliner paint, carefully draw the outlines of your shapes. Any mistakes should be wiped away immediately with a damp cloth.

4. Fill in the design using the watercolor brush. Leave to air-dry for four hours. Place in a cold oven and set to 160°C/325°F/mark 3. When the oven reaches this temperature, bake for thirty minutes. Turn the oven off and allow to cool in the closed oven.

YOU WILL NEED
Paper and pen for designing
Tube of outliner porcelain paint suitable for contact with food
Pot of porcelain paint suitable for contact with food
Fine watercolor paintbrushes
Plain white china

TIPS
- The paints I used are suitable for food use and are dishwasher-safe. However check carefully as brands vary. Other paints may require varnishing or have different baking instructions.
- If you want to use more than one color, the second color can be applied almost immediately as the paint dries in seconds.
- If you just want a border design, it may be easier to work on a rimmed plate rather than a rimless (coupe) shape.

FINISHING TOUCHES

"A home is not dead but living and like all living things, must obey the laws of nature by constantly changing."

Carl Larsson, Swedish artist

No time or inclination to renovate or decorate? Don't despair—retro style is still possible if you rethink, rearrange, and accessorize. Not only are '50s style vases, clocks, radios, and lights easily accessible and all the rage, but by choosing a stunning group of vases or a gorgeous lamp, you can dip your toe in the retro lido before diving in off the top board.

While '50s designs can easily be absorbed into any contemporary home, give a little thought to display. Items should have space to show themselves off, plus pieces always have more impact if several are arranged together. Arrange by color, shape, or style.

ABOVE Reminiscent of a Hepworth sculpture, this matte ceramic vase looks stunning positioned against the candy pink wall.

LEFT Typical of public clocks with their clear easy-to-read faces, such clocks are ideal for kitchens and home offices where the desire for efficiency is uppermost.

FAR LEFT Accentuate a collection of vintage objects by careful grouping. Don't be afraid to combine disparate elements: with retro style, the rule is "more is better."

Flowers—the blooming '50s

In the '50s flowers blossomed everywhere, perhaps as a peacetime reaction to the "Dig for Victory" war years when gardens turned into vegetable plots and tulips were replaced by turnips. Another influence was the growth of the "rural idyll" vision of suburbia. New houses were designed with a front and back garden and with increased leisure time available, gardening became a popular hobby, particularly for men.

Meanwhile flower arranging soared in popularity. Constance Spry, the doyenne of the oasis, was much in vogue, having designed the flowers for Queen Elizabeth's coronation in 1953. Her elegant and artistic arrangements were the perfect accomplishment for housewives aiming to be the hostess with the mostest. Spry wrote a number of books and set up a school of flower arranging in Surrey. If one could not afford to

buy fresh flowers year-round, the alternative was to use plastic flowers. These were popular in the '50s and were advertised as being fireproof and washable, so it could be perpetual summer in suburbia. Today, artificial flowers are no longer the poor relation to the fresh variety and look incredibly lifelike due to the subtle coloring of the petals, which are no longer plastic but artificial silk.

Using flowers and vases today is a much more relaxed affair than the formality of '50s arrangements. A stunning display can be created using vases of varying shapes, sizes, and materials, perhaps unified by the use of one or two colors. Don't hesitate at combining clear and colored glass with ceramics. If the grouping is dramatic enough, flowers or greenery may not even be necessary. For an authentic '50s feel, choose flowers with vintage appeal—roses, peonies, tulips, alliums,

marigolds, zinnias, lilies, and the most retro of the lot, the dahlia in all its gaudy glory.

Another reason for the popularity of flower arranging in the '50s was the abundance of vases in every style you can imagine—natural colors and textures of studio pottery, graphic sgraffito ceramics, and organic shapes in clear glass from Scandinavia were all common. Today the latter is highly collectible, but many original designs are still in production. Another classic shape of a slightly earlier era was Alvar Aalto's cloud vase, which echoed the rounded curves of coffee tables. For ceramic vases, a multitude of shapes were popular—everything from elongated hourglass forms with wasp waists to dumpy, rimless gourds and Hepworth-style vases with center holes. However, of all '50s vases, the most well-known style is probably the multicolored Murano glass from Italy. With their candy-

bright colors and organic forms, Murano vases can appear gaudy alongside the sophistication and elegance of Scandinavian glass. However, when displayed with restraint, Italian glass can look stunning. Needing no further decoration, they are best appreciated with excellent lighting but without flowers.

For an effective finishing touch to any retro interior, try any of the following:

- Play with scale and the '50s obsession with macro-micro combinations. Rather than displaying a bunch of lily stems in a single vase, chop off the oversized flower heads and display each individual bloom in a small glass next to a place setting. This not only looks sensational, it makes a few flowers go a long way.

- Alternatively, buy the longest stems possible of any dramatic flower such as an allium or leaf that has a very strong stem. Put two or

three of these blooms in a small, heavy-based glass vase (see page 86).

- Cut down stems on flowers such as tulips and pack densely into a vase, so the flower heads are packed together.

- Place a glass tumbler inside a larger vase. Fill the tumbler with water and flowers. Wrap clear, scrunched-up cellophane around the tumbler to hide it from view and fill the larger vase with cellophane. This way fewer blooms are needed.

- Don't limit yourself to vases. Conical polypropylene salad bowls look stunning filled with dahlias or peonies. To give support to these heavy blooms, tape a grid of sticky tape across the top of the bowl.

- On a smaller scale, put a couple of zinnia in a melamine cup and saucer in a contrasting color. Compact arrangements like this look

great on a bedside table or dotted along a mantelpiece.

- For a quick retro makeover for ordinary glass vases, wrap them tightly in wood-grained sticky-backed plastic. You do not need to stick the plastic to the vase. Simply overlap the edges and secure with double-sided tape.

FLOWERS Blooms with '50s appeal—peonies and parrot tulips all have bold shapes, and are available in dramatic colors. Real or artificial, the choice is yours.

VASES Contemporary glass vases inspired by Scandinavian glass of the '50s. Characterized by their combination of clear and colored glass (often called cased glass), and sinuous shapes, they look as good empty as full.

Clocks and radios

No retro home is complete without an authentic '50s clock and radio. The good news is that many are widely available. The classic styling has remained unchanged, but the technology has been brought up-to-date. The best '50s clocks are characterized by their large, clear, easy-to-read faces, reminiscent of clocks seen in public places such as stations and offices.

Depending on your style preferences, choose between rims made of enameled metal, chrome, and aluminium, or candy-colored plastic. Another '50s specialty is the kitchen or diner clock, sometimes with an integral timer (so don't hang too high on the wall where it will be out of reach).

Car design, space exploration, and science all influenced clock design in the '50s. Mantel clocks resembled dashboard instruments and novelty clocks were fitted into plastic "satellite" capsule casings or had cocktail cherry legs like a lunar landing module.

The ultimate '50s clock is surely the Ball Clock designed by George Nelson in collaboration with Isamu Noguchi and others. Extremely simple with a brushed metal case for the mechanism, the hours are defined by lacquered wood balls (sometimes multicolored) at the end of "cocktail sticks". Much copied, the original is still in production and fifty years on has lost none of its fun or visual impact.

ABOVE This funky plastic clock on its Saarinen style tulip base is perfect for a spaced-out bedroom.

LEFT The blue and green bedside clocks with their sleek chrome numbers are similar to speedometer instruments seen on car dashboards.

MUSIC ON THE MOVE

As a counter attack on the television, which gained popularity in the '50s, radio designs were given a style overhaul with new two-tone plastic casings and asymmetric designs. However, the other major catalysts were the combination of rock and roll music and teenagers with money to spend. This resulted in the popularity of transistor radios at the end of the decade and, as technology advanced, radios became smaller and more portable.

Of all the original brands, Roberts Revival Swing radios (see page 11) have achieved iconic status. Available in a range of perky and modern colors, the current model still has a traditional wooden cabinet as a base and is covered with a hand-crafted leather cover and leatherette trim. The combination of the handbag-style carry handle and jaunty logo make this design classic as much an item of desire now as it was when it was launched half a century ago. Available in over ten colors from sober "Bentley tan" to tomato red, why

stop with just one when you can choose a color to co-ordinate with the various color schemes in your home? However, if you would rather jive to the plastic fantastic, there is always the classic Bush TR2 design of 1959. This is still manufactured along with slightly more racy models strongly influenced by automobile styling.

ABOVE Appealing to all retro devotees, the Bush transistor is a must-have accessory.

Fifties kitsch—flashy, trashy, camp, and contemporary

Home accessories produced in the '50s were bright, often exotic in appearance, inexpensive, and like manna to customers who had been deprived of color and frivolity for many years. Many were manufactured using the "new materials" and technology developed during the war. Now seen as kitsch and of dubious taste, at the time they had widespread appeal for those wanting to give a modern and individual look to their home. These accessories were inexpensive throwaways at the time because they were produced in vast quantities, but are now becoming quite collectible.

Common ornaments in the '50s were the decorative wall plaques. Produced in plastic or plaster, they were highly colored and inexpensive in order to encourage regular purchases by their devoted collectors. Whether the plaques featured ballet dancers, poodles, exotic Orientals, or something equally bizarre, it is a '50s phenomenon that they always appeared as a "his and hers" pair. The exception to this pairing rule has to be the ultimate in '50s kitsch—the trio of flying ducks. Why three? Who knows?

A trio of flying ducks was the ultimate '50s ornament in suburbia. Their kitschness has come full circle and once again they are sought-after accessories.

This popular style was easy to acquire and was even more prevalent in the United States where there was a higher level of disposable income and not the same need to rebuild the basics of a home and family life after the war. One legacy of the war which had a direct effect on '50s' kitsch were the souvenirs soldiers brought home from the South Pacific Islands, China, and Japan. As a result, anything Oriental and Polynesian became all the rage throughout the '40s and '50s. This obsession was not confined to accessories, but also extended to rattan furniture and the use of bamboo as a popular motif for both fabrics and wallpapers.

HOLLYWOOD GLAMOR

Another influence on kitsch was the glamor of Hollywood—the spill-over effect into home accessories was demonstrated by a fondness for cocktail-hour items, flamingos, and animal prints. The Hollywood style of kitsch was often apparent in the entertaining side of home life—amazing ashtrays which were a celebration of smoking, "lazy Susan" revolving trays, plastic pineapple ice buckets, hostess trolleys, and frilly aprons ideal for popping on top of a cocktail frock when serving canapés to guests. Hardly minimalist chic, but definitely glitzy and glamorous.

GO FOR IT!

Every decade has its frivolous side and for consumers and homemakers in the '50s, there was an enormous pent-up demand for gaiety

and frivolity after the more somber '30s and '40s. Today, more than ever, homes are for living in and enjoying, so why not include a little bit of kitsch if it brings a smile to your face? The manufacturing of kitsch has never stopped, it's just been hidden under the carpet in recent years as homemakers have concentrated on minimalism, Shaker style, and clearly defined "Good Taste." However, like an embarrassing relation who turns up when least expected, kitsch has resurfaced with a number of specialty shops and mail order companies reveling in the loud, the tacky and the plastic items that we all love to hate.

So take a deep breath, mix yourself a Margarita, pop on a Hawaiian shirt and embrace the clashing colors and fakeness of it all. Then snap up the multicolored bead curtains, enamelled trays with Mexican beauties, polka dot beakers and palm tree fruit hammocks—how can you live without them?

BELOW LEFT Fun flower-shaped soaps have a place in the retro bathroom.

BELOW RIGHT The boomerang ashtray is a suitably off-beat companion to the cow hide rug.

ISAMU NOGUCHI (1904–1988)

There can be few homes and even fewer temporary apartments which do not have at least one globe paper lantern hanging from the ceiling. The majority of these ubiquitous lights are the cheap, mass-produced offspring of an original '50s design—the Akari light. Created in 1951 by Isamu Noguchi, a Japanese-American sculptor, they are based on Chochin, the egg-shaped paper lanterns used to illuminate night fishing boats. Of all Noguchi's design work and large public commissions, it is his small "intimate furnishings," as he termed them, which have received the greatest exposure.

In Japanese, Akari is the word for light (illumination). Noguchi chose this word for his designs as it also has the double meaning of weightlessness and fragility and his lamps in handmade mulberry paper (washi) certainly look fragile. The Akari range

was created as a result of a design brief from the mayor of Gifu City who wanted to revive the paper lantern industry in Nagoya province. Noguchi was briefed to design new lamps which would appeal to the American and European market.

In contrast to the cheap fringed and tasseled souvenir exports which had dominated the Nagoya factories after the war, Noguchi's designs referred back to the craftsmanship of the original Chochin lamps. Rather than candles, he electrified the lamps and designed a metal internal support, which made it possible for the lamps to be constructed in a variety of shapes as well as the original egg. The resulting Akari range successfully combined modern designs with papermaking, one of the indigenous crafts of Japan. As a sculptor, Noguchi explained:

"It [Akari] was an opportunity to extend the concept of sculpture from light reflective to translucent object."

The first designs were drawn by Noguchi in 1951. Prototypes were made by a number of manufacturers but Noguchi decided that one family firm, Ozeki, should manufacture his designs after a number of imitations started appearing on the market. Noguchi later returned to Japan to live for a year in 1952. During this period, he created further designs for Akari, ranging from pendants to table lamps and floor standing versions.

Whilst the inspiration for the original concept was a traditional lamp, many of the Akari designs have an unmistakable '50s feel—their bulbous shapes are in keeping with the biomorphic designs of the era. The floor and table lamps often perch on seemingly insubstantial metal legs ending in ball feet. All the lamps have the concentric bamboo (higo) spiral essential to their construction. This never-ending ring brings to mind the gaseous rings surrounding planets and the '50s preoccupation with outer space. As a sculptor, Noguchi's designs were also influenced by the organic sculptures of Brancusi in whose studio he had worked in the '20s. For the export market, Akari were made with plain white paper. Other versions included colored paper and lamps with geometric patterns.

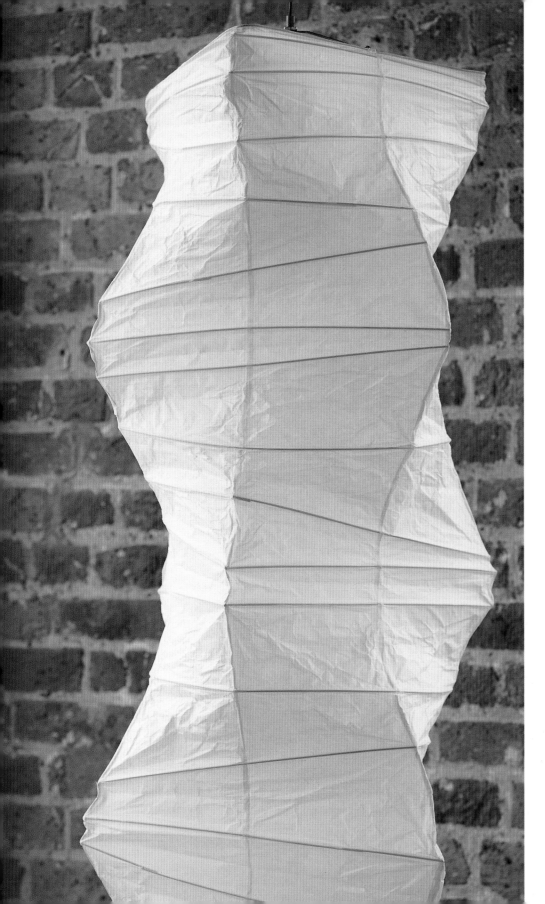

Akari received great commercial success although critical acclaim was more muted. Many of Noguchi's peers from the New York school of artists voiced their opinions that fine art and design could not be reconciled with mass production and commercial marketing and success. Despite this antipathy, Noguchi continued to expand the Akari range to over 100 shapes and the lamps are still manufactured by the Ozeki company according to Noguchi's original designs.

Almost half a century after the first Akari lamp was created, home retailer Habitat has taken up the washi and higo design baton. It has created a series of new paper lanterns called Osaki. Whilst Isamu Noguchi might not approve of this latest series of designs, regarding them as imitators, their easy availability and reasonable price would certainly appeal to his ideal of egalitarian design. Their sculptural quality and soft glowing light manage to transform the corner of even the most suburban home into a calm Japanese interior.

LEFT An original Akari floor lamp, the UF4-L8 stands an incredible seventy-four inches tall on slender tripod legs.

FAR LEFT Modern lamps inspired by Noguchi's designs of the '50s. These paper sculptures look especially good when grouped as a family.

Lighting

When you consider that not all homes in Britain had electricity at the start of the '50s, we have certainly come a long way in the past fifty years. There are many options when it comes to deciding on retro lighting. Trawling around junk shops and vintage stores may unearth some original wall lamps or a standard lamp with ball feet and a wrapped plastic raffia shade. Old lights should be re-wired (if in doubt, consult a qualified electrician). This is one safety area where 'vintage and quaint' are not desired adjectives. Alternatively, shop for twenty-first-century lamps with a feel for the past.

Any of the following design features will add instant retro appeal to a room:

- Paper lanterns to echo the classic designs of Isamu Noguchi (see previous pages).

- Small bendy desk lamps with oval enamel or plastic shades. Depending on your color preferences, you can select candy colored pastels, primaries, ivory, black, or brushed metal.

- Classic designs such as Poul Henningsen's 1954 design, the Artichoke pendant. Made from overlapping steel plates, this clever design meant that the light was evenly distributed and reflected, but the bulb was not visible. This '50s take on the classic chandelier has spawned various imitations in other materials. Another Henningsen design, the PH5 pendant, is made from discs and cups of enameled aluminium and, like many '50s designs, strongly refers to space craft but without descending into kitsch.

- However, if kitsch is what you want, choose a '50s style chandelier, without a crystal drop in site. Hang a stunning version with plastic drops somewhere where it will catch the light.

- If that isn't enough kitsch, top it off with potted cacti lights or strings of novelty party lights in the shapes of parrots, beer mugs, or tropical fruit. Barbecue anyone?

- Look for designs by Achille and Pier Giacomo Castiglioni. These Italian brothers produced some excellent designs in the '50s, which still look contemporary today. One classic model is the Luminator uplighter of 1954, a leggy and slender design on tripod legs.

- Classic anglepoise lamps in brushed metal, ivory, or black. Unlike the '50s, many of today's designs will feature halogen bulbs for more effective task lighting.

- Any space age design (see the Sputnik lamp on page 11). Look out for rocket-shaped translucent glass shades on slender metal bases, plastic satellite lamps, sparkling lunar lamps resting on a chrome stand. Many halogen lights, whether recessed ceiling spots or low voltage track systems attached to suspended wires, fit the retro style.

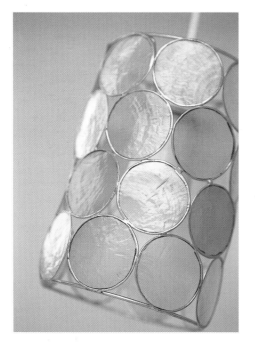

FAR LEFT This delicate lamp with textured glass discs makes a pretty addition to a pastel room.

LEFT Elegantly understated, this pendant made from interwoven strips of natural cotton makes an ideal light for a Scandinavian-style interior.

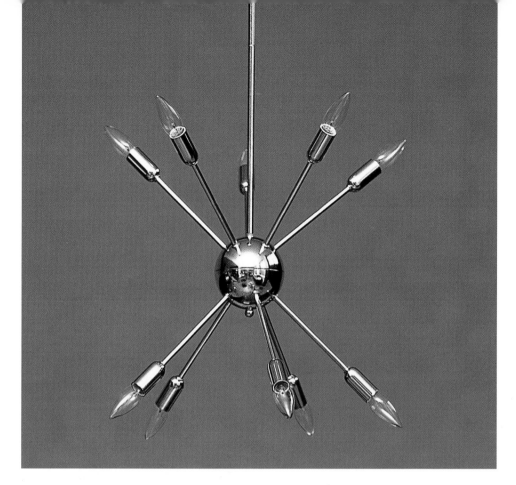

Whatever style of lamp you choose, strike a balance between the different types of lighting in each room. You should have a balance of ambient (general) lighting, task lighting for work areas including the kitchen, accent lighting for highlighting objects or wall displays and lighting that is purely decorative.

LEFT The pièce de résistance when it comes to a central pendant light, is the chromed atomic chandelier.

BELOW With its three-legged chrome stand, this sparkly table lamp can provide a touch of disco glamour to any dark corner.

- Chunky dark wood bases in simple shapes, topped with a white or linen drum shade.

- Ceramic bases in any shapes similar to vases, e.g. hour glass, sinuous, Hepworth (holey).

- Anything with three metal legs and ball feet for authentic cocktail-cherry appeal. Usually topped with a polypropylene shade.

- Natural wooden or metal bases topped with a rattan, raffia, or cane shade. This style is a natural complement to a Scandinavian style interior. Try making your own (see pages 126–127). Modern classics such as Michael Sodeau's rattan floor lamp stands as tall as a person and has the shape of an elegant tapering bottle.

- Spun aluminium pendants of various shapes and sizes, ideal for diner kitchens.

- Kitsch his and hers matching lamp bases. Usually made of plaster, these can be huge. Choose an equally impressive shade to balance the impact of the base. Look out for lamp bases in the shapes of matadors, harlequins, exotic dancers, or Hollywood starlets.

- Twin wall lights, often featuring gently curved arms in brushed metal and frosted glass conical-shaped shades.

- Children's night lamps in frosted white glass. In the '50s there was a vogue for "television lamps"—very low wattage lamps which were popped on top of the television set. Today, such subtle lights would look far more funky sitting on the floor and partnered with a classic Jack or Spike lamp by Tom Dixon.

RAFFIA-TRIMMED LAMPSHADE

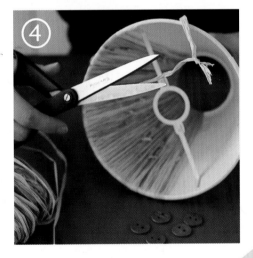

Take an ordinary light and turn it into something decidedly more stylish with a new raffia jacket.

1. Using a tape measure and pencil, divide the bottom of the lampshade into twelve even sections to mark the position of the curtain weights. Polish the weights with white spirit and a soft cloth to enhance their shine and hide any scratches.

2. Pull out and cut off a length of raffia from the bundle. Secure inside the shade at the top with a small piece of masking tape. Start to wrap quite tightly around the shade from top to bottom.

3. When you reach each pencil mark, thread the raffia through a curtain weight, making sure it is level with the bottom rim of the shade.

4. When you reach the end of the raffia, cut off another length and knot the two lengths together, trimming any surplus. Make sure any joins are hidden inside the shade. Continue wrapping around the shade. Finish off by tying the raffia to the gimble in order to secure.

YOU WILL NEED
Tape measure
Pencil
Plain white or cream lampshade (size to fit lamp base)
Twelve curtain weights
White spirit
Soft cloth
Bundle of natural raffia
Masking tape
Scissors

TIPS
- Covering a lampshade will give a soft, ambient light. For a brighter light, cover a metal lamp ring with raffia.
- Always use the correct wattage of bulb recommended for the lampshade.
- As an alternative to the curtain weight trimming, glue a braid trim to the lower edge of the shade.

THIS PAGE An original 50s' kitchen looks as good as new with a fresh coat of vanilla paint and gleaming chrome handles. Contemporary kitchen equipment happily sits side by side with junk shop finds.

PUTTING IT ALL TOGETHER

"Whatever you can do or dream you can do, begin it.
Boldness has genius, power and magic in it."

Goethe

The most terrifying or exciting part of any decorative scheme is starting out. Where to start and how to combine it all are the two most common questions facing any decorator. Add into the equation the fact that you want to incorporate a retro look and the choices can be overwhelming. However, help is at hand. Follow the ideas in this chapter and suddenly retro chic is easy to achieve. The first thing to remember is that the retro look encompasses all the following elements: fun, frilly, floral, simple, sophisticated, natural, organic, metallic, homely, space age, modern, color, monochrome. So chose the elements right for you and start experimenting.

WHERE TO START?

The chances are that you already have some possessions to incorporate into a new decorative scheme. With a change of emphasis, it is often quite easy to switch the mood of a room with color and accessories. However, if you are starting from scratch, a good beginning is to pick a favorite possession as inspiration and use this to build on. This can be anything from a junk-shop plate to a to-die-for chair by a contemporary designer. An excellent technique used by many designers is to use a storyboard to build up a

LEFT Modern wallpaper swatches in retro colors and simple graphic designs.

BELOW Fifties paint charts with suggestions for color scheming.

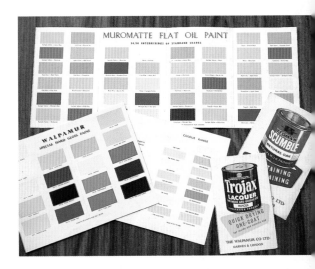

collection of ideas. This is a good focal point for all your ideas and allows you to audition different elements such as fabrics, furniture styles, and paint colors in a manageable format.

MAKING A STORYBOARD

First buy a piece of white mount board or foam board from an art shop at least poster-size. Foam board is particularly good as it allows you to pin items to it and then rearrange them as your ideas change.

Look closely at your "inspiration"—what colors and patterns does it include? What shape and texture is it? And what style—fun, cozy, funky, classic, modern, homespun? Pick up paint charts or sample pots from hardware stores, collect flooring, fabric and trimming swatches, and tear pictures that appeal to you from magazines and newspapers. It is also a good idea to take a photo of the room or any pieces of furniture that are to be included, and add these to the board.

Leave the board in the room to be decorated so that you can check the scheme at different times of the day and in different lights. By gathering everything, you will soon see which elements gel and which jar.

When choosing paint colors, always check the actual paint color rather than a printed paint chart. So once you have narrowed down the color choices to three or four, buy sample pots and paint a small amount onto a sheet of white paper, which you can attach to the storyboard. Paint the rest onto larger sheets of paper, which can then be pinned up in the room and "lived with" over several days.

It is important to look at the colors in both natural and artificial light—blue can appear fresh in daylight but quite cold at night if the lighting is wrong. While it may seem extravagant buying so many tiny pots of paint, in the long run this will save money (and time), as you can be sure to get the color right the first time. Also remember that once you see the paint over a large area, it will appear darker or more intense than the sample on the paint chart, hence the importance of the painted samples.

RETRO WITH ZEST AND A TWIST

The board below shows a kitchen/dining room scheme based on vintage china. The owner already had a laminate table and chairs, which were to be included. The room had to fulfill a variety of needs and the decoration budget was relatively small. The resulting scheme successfully lightens and brightens the room, and provides a colorful foil to the ceramics. It also shows how retro style can be incorporated into houses of all sizes and ages—in this case a small Victorian terrace is given a zesty "retro with a twist" treatment.

BELOW Vintage colors. Against a background of fresh turquoise and creamy white, the clean lines of plywood and laminated furniture stand out. Bright accents of paint color are to be used on a modular MDF storage unit. Fifties fabric scraps are sewn into napkins, and cardboard boxes provide ample storage for everything from cutlery to bank statements.

If the thought of bright retro colors has you reaching for the can of magnolia, remember that just like Marie Peppercorn's ceramics on page 108, paint can be applied in blocks, such as an alcove or a bold stripe down half a wall. Alternatively, keep the walls very subtle in an off-white, and paint the floor instead. Paint manufacturers now make paints suitable for covering all types of surfaces including wood, concrete, and vinyl. Experiment with a stenciled pattern in a simple graphic design (see pages 40–41 for details).

SCANDINAVIAN MODERN

A second scheme shows how flexible retro is as a style—a '40s apartment in Gothenburg uses natural tones and textures to create a modern yet comfortable interior. Vintage accessories and furniture are effortlessly mixed with contemporary designs. This is the essence of '50s Scandinavian style—natural wood and ply for furniture and floors, teamed with refined, comfortable furniture designs. Off-white walls visually enlarge and lighten the rooms and make the most of the limited northern light. Simple window treatments in heavy, textured, handwoven, slubbed cottons and linens, or bold, abstract designs keep out the cold. Finally, a few classic ceramic, or glass accessories are chosen to complete the comfortable "less is more" interior.

This look can be achieved in almost any age or style of house. Its organic simplicity makes it easy to add to the scheme over time. Vintage furniture sourced from junk shops and antique dealers lives happily with items from modern Scandinavian companies such as IKEA, as there is a common denominator of wood, rattan, chrome, and webbing.

Always check the type of flooring lurking underneath your carpet. Floorboards, parquet, or modern laminates all complement Scandinavian decorating styles. The one paint tip is not to use pure brilliant white on the walls—it looks too harsh in the colder light of the northern hemisphere. Instead, choose one of the many other whites available, or a contrasting color such as green, which sits well with this natural look. Lighting styles can be mixed, but keep to clean, functional designs, and white, wood, plastic, and metal finishes.

ABOVE Calm and collected. The emphasis here is on texture and contrasts—wooden floors covered by sheepskins; subtle woven upholstery and curtain fabrics contrast with soft fleece and corduroy throws and suede cushions. Chalky paint colors are used with restraint, and accessories are chosen with care to enhance the feeling of space and light.

CUSTOMIZING

Although the later '50s were an affluent era, especially in Europe, the early years were a time of making do, improvising, and customizing. Nowadays, although we do not have to make curtains out of black-out material, or furniture from war-surplus aluminium, there is still an opportunity to create an individual home without a massive cash outlay, rather an investment of time, ideas, and lateral thinking.

The majority of the following ideas can be tackled by any novice. Practical information is readily available from home-design magazines and television programs. Many home improvements stores have specialists who can assist with advice on projects and products.

- Rummage through the racks at charity shops for knitwear. Sweaters and cardigans can be converted to cozy cushion covers at a fraction of the cost of those available through design stores. Look for Arans, cable knits, Fair Isles, or pastel twinsets. Simply cut to the size of your cushion pads,

remembering to overlock or zigzag the edges to prevent the unravelling of rows. Sweater cushions require zips, while cardigan cushions can use the front buttoning as the fastening. If the colors are not right or are faded, simply dye them.

- Vintage fabric scraps can be sewn into shoe bags (far prettier than cardboard boxes), or larger remnants into laundry bags. Just turn over a hem at the top edge, stitch around the remaining sides and thread a pajama-type drawstring cord through the top hem, knotting the ends together.

- Revel in the '50s soap suds look and cover a traditional wooden ironing board (available inexpensively from IKEA) with a bold 1950s print. Attach with drawing pins or a drawstring, depending on the board's construction. Remember to prewash the fabric to check for color fastness. Complete the look by sewing a quirky clothespin bag.

- If you manage to find a vintage patchwork quilt, it may have worn holes in places or have frayed edges if it has been well used. Instead of trying to patch, and provided it is not a valuable antique, cut it up to create smaller throws, cushions, hot-water bottle covers, or small quilted hearts that can be filled with lavender and hung in a closet.

- For felted cushions, put old wool jumpers in hot soapy water and rub vigorously. The wool fibers will felt together. The same

ABOVE Vintage style needn't cost a fortune—all it needs is a fresh outlook.

LEFT Get out the sewing machine, and pick up the knitting needles, for an evening of patching, knitting, and cushion-making.

effect can be achieved with less effort in the washing machine on a hot wash—now is the chance to recycle those washing disasters into retro wonders!

- Re-cover '50s junk-shop upholstery. Remember to check the padding on chairs and sofas, as a lot of retro upholstery used foam, which can deteriorate. However if the frame is still sound, it is worth repadding and covering in a contemporary fabric. Look for sofa and chairs with legs or divan beds, which were popular in the '50s and mass-produced.

- Utility furniture can still be found quite cheaply. The designs often have a quiet, simple modernism as they were based on the best of '30s European designs, and work well in any Scandinavian-style interior. Bring up to date by liming the wood, covering the tops of tables with galvanized

metal, linen, or canvas if badly marked, and replacing the handles.

- Small '50s wooden kitchen tables, often with enameled tops, can always be squeezed into a home. All that is needed is a fresh coat of paint and some new baize for the cutlery drawer. For a different look, spray the wood frame in a metallic paint, cover the top with PVC fabric and attach a set of castors to the legs to make the furniture more flexible.

- No '50s kitchen was complete without a free-standing kitchen cabinet. These cabinets provide a quirky alternative to built-in storage, and can provide storage for linens, toys or . . . kitchenware.

- Update your kitchen by painting existing units. Eggshell paint (often called satinwood or semigloss) works well on melamine or wooden doors. For a funky retro look, paint each door a different color. Customize with new handles.

- Medium density fiberboard (MDF) furniture can be bought as "blanks" ready to paint from a variety of companies. Especially good are the delicate Gustavian-style dressing tables, mirrors, and screens. When painted in soda-fountain colors, they become ideal partners to floral bed linen in a retro boudoir.

- MDF is easy to cut into curvy shapes (see pages 80–81 for details). Using a jigsaw, cut curvaceous shelving—ideal for displaying the plump curves of mid-century ceramics.

ABOVE Jazz up juice glasses with glass paint and jolly patterns. Odd glasses can be used in the bathroom as toothbrush mugs.

LEFT Cover your ironing board with '50s-style fabric.

QUICK ACCESSORIES FOR INSTANT RETRO STYLE

- Make storage fun by covering shoe boxes and hatboxes with fabric, sticky-backed plastic, or wallpaper. The humble shoe box can revel in its new gingham, mock teak, or rosebud attire. Metal handle plates can be bought from DIY stores or ironmongers.

- For an instant retro art gallery, stretch a metal curtain wire between two walls at eye level. Onto this peg black and white photos scrounged from your family archives. Alternatively, attach the wire higher up the wall and have the photos laminated at a copy shop to give them large invisible frames. Other ideas for laminating include vintage knitting patterns, records sleeves from 45s, or pages from a '50s comic such as *Eagle*.

- Cover thick foam board or soft board with utility fabrics such as black-and-white ticking or solid-color felt for a smart accent in a home office or kitchen. Stretch the fabric tightly over the board and staple to the back. Lengths of webbing can be stretched across in a diamond pattern so that essential documents and photos can be easily stored or displayed.

- Just as the '50s embraced new materials, retro devotees should be inspired by sheets of polypropylene (a popular late '90s material), bought from specialist stationers or art shops. They come in many colors, and can be used to create modern retro lampshades when curved around a lamp holder. Look for ideas in home stores—they are using polypropylene for wall and table lights, and accessories as it can be cut, bent, or folded into a variety of shapes.

SOURCING THE RETRO LOOK

This book is intended to be a taster for retro style. To learn more about '50s design, refer to any of the books listed at the end of the books, spend time in your local library or visit auction houses when they are having viewing days for mid-century sales (usually a mixture of furniture, textiles, lighting, and accessories). Also talk to friends and family who were born in the early '30s, as memories of first homes are often quite vivid. If you are really lucky you may be able to acquire some authentic retro pieces for free, as people learn of your interest in the period!

Many '50s pieces are still in production today with the designs essentially unchanged, although the technology or materials used have been brought up to date. Refer to the comprehensive. In home style magazines look out for details of shops and manufacturers who deal in authentic retro (old pieces made in the '50s) and retro-style items (products manufactured today inspired by original '50s designs). As e-commerce becomes a way of life in the twenty-first century, surf the Internet for Web sites connected to '50s designs. Often it is the links to other sites that are the most rewarding feature of Web sites. A few are listed, but remember that new sites come online daily.

Absorbing a retro style into your home is relatively easy as you can pick and choose those elements you find most appealing. Vintage furniture can happily live with modern designs if there is some common denominator such as materials used—wood, chrome, leather. Accessories and paint can pep up an otherwise nondescript interior, even choosing the right type of vase or flower can add a touch of retro to a corner of a room.

The main thing to remember is what makes up retro style—appreciation of contemporary designs, a willingness to experiment with "modern" colors and materials, making the most of living spaces, a "make do and mend" attitude, and a relaxed and casual approach to interiors. It's not about spending vast sums of money (although of course that is possible), it is more about a positive and optimistic attitude to interiors, designs, and enjoyment of living in your home.

LEFT A single classic design, such as these Eames' chairs adds mid-century modern style to an otherwise traditional home.

THIS PAGE Encompassing retro style in a subtle way, with '50s colors, motifs, and a few offbeat accessories.

FROSTED GLASS VASE

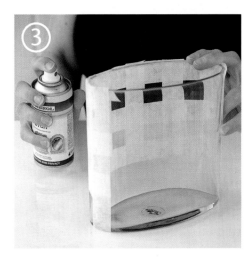

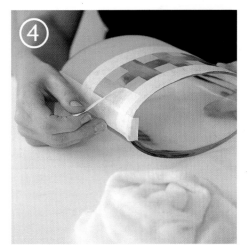

Design a graphic frosted vase which looks as good empty as it does full of blooms.

1. For inspiration and ideas, look at retro-style fabric or wallpaper patterns featuring simple checks and stripes. Wash and dry the vase to ensure it is free from dust or grease.

2. Using lengths of tape, mask off areas of the vase which are to remain clear. Even if you are frosting just one side, make sure the sides are protected from stray frosting powder.

3. In a well ventilated room and with the table surface protected, spray the vase in a gently sweeping movement, keeping the aerosol at a distance of 6in., following the manufacturer's instructions. Repeat on the other side of the vase if desired.

4. Leave the vase to dry for at least one hour, then carefully peel off the tape to reveal the frosted design.

YOU WILL NEED
Masking tape or Magic Tape
Scissors
Glass vase
Old newspaper or a cloth to protect the table
Aerosol of frosting solution

TIPS
- For a more elaborate design, enlarge words (in a '50s-style typeface) on a photocopier. Trace onto stencil paper and cut out with a craft knife. Attach the stencil to the glass with Spray Mount.
- As a rule, only one coat of the frosting solution is needed. The more coats you apply, the harder it is to achieve crisp, clean edges on your design.
- If there is some "bleeding" at the edges, use a craft knife to scrape away the excess, taking care not to scratch the glass. Lighter fluid and a soft cloth can also remove mistakes; however, this tends to remove a lot of frosting.
- As well as vases, you can use the solution on glass frames, doors, windows or mirrors. The solution used here is food- and dishwasher-safe, but you should check for the brand you are using.

CREDITS

The author and publisher would like to thank the following companies for generously loaning products for photography. All photography by Sue Wilson unless otherwise credited.

Aero: photo p. 72; After Noah: metal beds pp 2, 96, Bakelite table p. 37, bedside cabinet p. 63; Amtico: Terrazzo flooring pp 19, 22, 30, 43; Aria: purple table p. 33, turquoise table p. 78; Artisan Curtain Rails: curtain pole p. 89; Bhs: polypropylene lamp p. 21, pastel lampshade p. 124; Bliss: atomic clock p. 44; Brats: TV clock pp 18, 43, bedside clocks p. 118, atomic chandelier p. 125, sparkle lamp p. 125; Bush: radio/cassette player pp 16, 19, antique radio pp 40, 119; Cath Kidston: roseprint bed linen pp 2, 88, 91, patchwork cushion p. 96, floral cushion p. 132, gingham fabric pp 13, 133; The Conran Shop: plywood table p. 23; Crown Paints: paint charts p. 129; Dalsouple: rubber flooring pp 80, 106; Dualit: pastel toasters pp 105, 111; Eclectics Blinds: photos pp 35, 82, 86; Environment: plastic beakers p. 19, bottle rack p. 21, plastic cutlery p. 21; Ever trading: roseprint tray p. 37, roseprint chairs p. 79; Fablon: woodeffect plastic pp 43, 102, 105, 112, 119; Fritz Hansen: Jacobsen chairs pp 4, 76, photo p. 77; Grimes & Co: checked blankets p. 93, woven lampshade p. 124; Guzzini: photos p. 111; Habitat: paper lights pp 4, 122, Day chairs pp 10, 68; laminate chairs p. 24, sgraffito tableware p. 47 top & bottom, Day curtains p. 62, Day bed linen p. 63, white table p. 68; Hobby Craft: turquoise vases p. 30; IKEA: square plates p. 8, blue fabric p. 8, rattan chair p. 23, blue armchair p. 69, square tables pp 87, 132, printed voile p. 87; Inside: '50s sideboards pp 7, 76, '50s desk pp 70, 134, plastic clock p. 118, Eames chairs p. 134; Isokon Plus: plywood stool p. 22, magazine rack p. 22, plywood tray p. 46; Jerrys Homestore: toast rack pp 99, 111, honey bear p. 101, printed glass p. 102, syrup drizzler p. 102, straw dispenser p. 102, diner mugs p. 103, milkshake glasses p. 105, citrus juicer p. 110, photo p. 100; Kitschen Sync: diner stool p. 19, scrubbing brushes p. 21, polkadot beakers p. 21, kitchen clock p. 30, kitchen scales p. 32, metal colander p. 32, stacking glasses p. 102, electric blender p. 104, flower soaps p. 121; Knoll International: chairs p. 38, photos pp 12, 68, 75; The Laundry/Gloria Nicol: photos pp 31, 52, 90; *Livingetc* magazine: photos pp 14, 36, 98, 128 (Peter Aprahamian), p. 73 (W. Heinze), pp 92, 114, 135 (L. Hind), pp 66, 74, 84 (H. Wilson); LSA International: turquoise vase pp 3, 78, red vase, pp 7, 37, 76, blue vases pp 18, 38, 116, 117; Marie Peppercorn: photos p. 109, Morphy Richards: flat iron pp 13, 133, retro toaster p. 17, retro kettle p. 110; Ocean: glass table p. 3, magazine rack p. 62, rattan table p. 126; Purves and Purves: tissuebox cover p. 21, sugar/sauce boat p. 21, baby bowls, p. 21, plywood chairs pp 28, 126, ketchup dispenser p. 101; Repeat Repeat: printed mugs pp 48, 104; Robert Opie Collection: photo p. 49; Roberts Radio: lilac radio p. 11, yellow radio p. 50; Sanderson: photo p. 53; Scottwood of Nottingham: photo p. 138; SCP: butterfly stool p. 23, Eames Hang-it-All p. 42, Eames chair p. 70; Sia UK: fake flowers pp 116, 117; Simon Pengelly: photo p. 24 bottom; Stepan Tertsakian; calf hide rug pp 79, 121, Mongolian lamb rug p. 118; twentytwentyone: Noguchi lampshade p. 123; Visto: patterned cushions pp 10, 95, patterned curtains p. 23, wall lights pp 26, 76, foreign ceramics p. 45, patterned fabric p. 46, illuminated globes pp 64, 70, '50s chairs pp 64, 96, striped vase p. 80; Wood Bros Furniture: Perspex tables pp 18, 79.

Quotes from interview with Dominic Lutyens, *The Independent* 14 November 1998

I would like to thank the following people: Ljiljana Baird at MQ Publications for having faith in my writing abilities; Alison Moss and Gillian Haslam, both excellent editors, for their ability to boost my confidence and to keep me on schedule; the superb creative team—Sue Wilson, photographer, Beth Evans, stylist, and Liz Lewis, designer—for helping to turn this concept into reality with minimum fuss and maximum ideas; and my family and friends for their support.

Marion Haslam

Further reading

Marga Anstett-Jansen, *Knoll Design*, Knoll International 1998

John Baeder, *Diners*, Harry N. Abrams, Inc 1978

Mary Banham and Bevis Hillier, *A Tonic to the Nation*, Thames & Hudson 1976 (out of print)

David Bond, *The Guiness Guide to 20th Century Homes*, Guiness Books 1984 (out of print)

Gideon Bosker, John Gramstad, Michele Mancini, *Fabulous Fabrics of the 50s*, Chronicle Books 1992

Jan Boxshall, *Good Housekeeping: Every Home Should Have One*, Ebury Press 1997 (out of print)

Mark Burns and Louis Di Bonis, *Fifties Homestyle*, Thames & Hudson 1988

Richard Chamberlain, *From Austerity to Affluence*, Merrell Holberton 1997

Christies, *Scandinavian Design*, Christies International 1999

Sarah Colombo, *The Chair*, Aurum Press 1997

Cherie and Kenneth Fehrman, *Postwar Interior Design*, Van Nostrand Reinhold 1980

Juliet Gardiner, *From the Bomb to the Beatles*, Collins & Brown 1999

Bevis Hillier, *The Style of the Century*, The Herbert Press 1983

Thomas Hine, *Populuxe*, Bloomsbury 1990

Lesley Jackson, *The New Look Design in the Fifties*, Thames & Hudson 1998

Sylvia Katz, *Classic Plastics*, Thames & Hudson 1984

Catherine McDermott, *C20th Design*, Carlton Books 1999

Graham McLaren, *Ceramics of the 1950s*, Shire Publications 1997

Madeleine Marsh, *Collecting The 1950s*, Miller's/Reed 1997

Robert Opie, *The 1950s Scrapbook*, New Cavendish Books 1998

Christopher Pearce, *Fifties Source Book*, Grange Books 1998 (out of print)

Project index

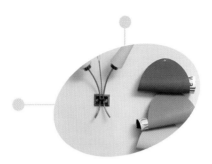

INDEX

First published in the United States of America in 2000
By Universe Publishing
A Division of Rizzoli International Publications, Inc.
300 Park Avenue South
New York, NY 10010

Text © 2000 Marion Haslam

00 01 02 / 10 9 8 7 6 5 4 3 2 1

Printed in Italy

Library of Congress Cataloging-in-Publication Data

Haslam Marion.
    Retro style : the '50's look for today's home / Marion Haslam ; photography by Sue Wilson.
        p. cm.
    ISBN 0-7893-0403-1 (pbk.)
    I. Interior decoration—United States—History—20th century. 2. Nineteen fifties. I.
    Title.

NK2004 .H38 2000
747.2'0495—dc21   00-020546